"Effectively skewering a central fallacy of the age, David Dark argues that at the deepest level no one is more or less religious than anyone else. With his premise granted, new avenues for ownership, responsibility and a renewed attentiveness to all we say, do and think arise. *Life's Too Short to Pretend You're Not Religious* is a call to consciousness and the compassion that accompanies the sacred insight that the whole world is kin and everything belongs."
Richard Rohr, O.F.M., Center for Action and Contemplation

"Brace yourself. Our bold conceits, wishful thinking and soothing sobriquets on the abolition of religion and the end of faith are set on a collision course thanks to David Dark's luminous reckonings with the real. The result is a shock of recognition: life more abundant awaits us only in the deep immersions of togetherness with others. Here alone are the comedy and chaos that define the human condition and lead us gently or not into the strange new world of grace. *Life's Too Short to Pretend You're Not Religious* is an irresistible triumph."
Charles Marsh, Commonwealth Professor of Religious Studies, University of Virginia, author of *Strange Glory: A Life of Dietrich Bonhoeffer*

"Don't let an aversion toward that radioactive word dissuade you. *Life's Too Short to Pretend You're Not Religious* is a bracing manifesto for modern people and an optimism-infused love song to humanity. David Dark calls us to pay better, more generous attention to our own lives and the lives of others."
Sara Zarr, National Book Award finalist, author of *The Lucy Variations*

"David Dark is one of the most important prophetic voices of our day. *Life's Too Short to Pretend You're Not Religious* is another beautiful demonstration of the winsome way in which he unsettles our language and our imagination. Not content to unravel the basic fabric of our existence, Dark reweaves the fibers into a rich and vibrant vision of the flourishing religious life for which we were created."
C. Christopher Smith, coauthor of *Slow Church* and founding editor of *The Englewood Review of Books*

"David Dark has a request for all of us. Stop thinking of being religious as passivity. Stop thinking of it as participation in something monolithic, intractable and stagnated by centuries of routine. In his new book, he asks us instead to find religion all around us: in music, television, books and film. In doing so, he reimagines being religious as a collective action open to all and demonstrates that in a time skeptical of religion, it can be a source of meaningful work and lifegiving pleasure and joy—and even of change."
Kaya Oakes, College Writing Programs, University of California, Berkeley

"I am so very grateful for this book, which, among other things, demonstrates that answering 'Jedi' or 'Toni Morrison' when asked for your religious affiliation is a perfectly legitimate response to that question—thereby arguing us into another definition of what it means to be alive to wonder and mystery. And at a time in our culture when we seem to prefer our 'dialogues' to be conducted behind well-defended barricades from which we lob Twitter grenades, David Dark shows us that there could be another way to live with each other and speak with each other. Each sentence here is graced with a wisdom, humor and humility that can't help but inspire us to be a little less suspicious of each other and to hope a little bit more—and if that isn't a rare gift of prophecy, I don't know what is. Also, he writes like an unprintable word, and for that I am glad."

Carlene Bauer, author of *Frances and Bernard* and *Not That Kind of Girl*

"Having just finished David Dark's new book, I want to buy stock in Religion Unlimited, meaning that David helps us see why pronouncing religion dead or dying is terribly short-sighted. The writing is muscular yet graceful, and the content is wise and insightful. You couldn't ask more from a book . . . and you couldn't ask for a more important subject."

Brian D. McLaren, author, speaker, activist

"David Dark is one of our most astute and necessary cultural critics. His work gracefully opens new doors of understanding and breaks down barriers between secular and non-, and it puts a lot of old mythology out to pasture with a daring affirmation at the heart of his radical critique. *Life's Too Short* refreshingly ropes everyone in, insisting that we're all in it together. We forget that."

Jessica Hopper, author of *The First Collection of Criticism by a Living Female Rock Critic*

"Prepare to have idols smashed. David Dark renders futile the cherished modern ambition to opt out of human religiosity; religion, rather, is a road we can make by walking with open eyes and informed minds. No marvels of progress can save us from being heretics and holy fools, or prophets, seers and miracle workers. Dark helps us recognize these characters (and more) on the radio, in a dreary parking lot and within ourselves."

Nathan Schneider, columnist for *America* magazine, author of *God in Proof* and *Thank You, Anarchy*

Life's too short to pretend you're not religious

David Dark

IVP Books

An imprint of InterVarsity Press
Downers Grove, Illinois

InterVarsity Press
P.O. Box 1400, Downers Grove, IL 60515-1426
ivpress.com
email@ivpress.com

InterVarsity Press® is the book-publishing division of InterVarsity Christian Fellowship/USA®, a movement of students and faculty active on campus at hundreds of universities, colleges and schools of nursing in the United States of America, and a member movement of the International Fellowship of Evangelical Students. For information about local and regional activities, visit intervarsity.org.

While any stories in this book are true, some names and identifying information may have been changed to protect the privacy of individuals.

Cover design: Cindy Kiple
Interior design: Beth McGill

ISBN 978-0-8308-4446-3 (print)
ISBN 978-0-8308-9942-5 (digital)

Printed in the United States of America ∞

Library of Congress Cataloging-in-Publication Data

Names: Dark, David, 1969-
Title: Life's too short to pretend you're not religious / David Dark.
Description: Downers Grove : InterVarsity Press, 2016. | Includes bibliographical references.
Identifiers: LCCN 2015036062 | ISBN 9780830844463 (hardcover : alk. paper)
Subjects: LCSH: Philosophical theology. | Apologetics.
Classification: LCC BT40 .D37 2016 | DDC 230--dc23
LC record available at http://lccn.loc.gov/2015036062

P	21	20	19	18	17	16	15	14	13	12	11	10	9	8	7	6	5	4	3	2	1
Y	33	32	31	30	29	28	27	26	25	24	23	22	21	20	19	18	17	16			

For Rachel Masen

This goes out to those for whom:

Religion is violence backed by divinity.

Religion is a backward step in human evolution.

Religion kills joy.

Religion is why you can't talk to your family.

Religion is the state of being hopelessly stuck.

Religion is brainwash.

Religion is the old relative who can't change his mind and won't change the subject.

Religion is a cage around reason.

Religion is the thorn in the side of common sense.

Religion will not house complexity, mystery, the unknown or contradiction.

Religion represents death of the imagination, invention and seeing yourself in someone else.

Religion is the elaborate disguise for Fear that gets him a seat at the table of survival.

This *also* goes out to those for whom:

Religion is peace backed by divinity.

Religion is a forward step in human evolution.

Religion gives joy.

Religion is the call to somehow honor and revere your family.

Religion sings songs to the silenced and forgotten.

Religion illuminates the invisible threads of cosmic connection.

Religion is the moral memory of humankind.

Religion is an ancient intelligence summoning us to choose humility over hubris and love over fear.

Religion dresses the wounds of alienation, isolation, oppression, desertion, haste and hierarchy.

Religion is the lexicon of mystery.

Religion brings the dead back to tell stories.

Religion is the library of love and longing, candor and liveliness.

Contents

Introduction

Religion happens

It wasn't their fault, it wasn't her fault.
It wasn't even a matter of fault.

Elmore Leonard, *The Switch*

"NO ONE DOESN'T BELIEVE IN GOD as much as I do," a slightly intoxicated friend assured me as we huddled together in a busy restaurant one Saturday evening. I knew we were in for an extraordinary conversation. Sometimes this kind of thing comes up when I'm asked what I do.

When I could honestly call myself a high school English teacher, my responses generated less heat. Someone might recite Shelley's "Ozymandias," recall a beloved teacher or ask for a reading recommendation, but it rarely took a turn for the intensely personal. Now that I work with undergraduates, they want to know what it is I teach, exactly.

Religion.

But what classes?

Bible. World religions.

And now we're awash in the prickliest of questions—the existence of God. The moment my friend asserted his superlative disbelief in God did not come out of the blue. We'd been at it a while on the subject of weird religious backgrounds (his and mine), life after death, music, science and all the different things people say *the Bible says*. I suspect I surprised him a little when I noted that we read it badly until we learn to read it as a collection and that, wherever one lands on the question of the existence of God, the Bible's likely as good as it gets when it comes to challenging everyday injustice.

He wanted to know if I believed it, and I assured him that I did. But I described my love for the Bible with so many seemingly diverse points of entry that he seemed a little taken aback: Kurt Vonnegut's devotion to the Sermon on the Mount, the ethical momentum set in motion within human societies by the prophets, the vision of beloved community in the civil rights movement and my own dependence on the wisdom of my incarcerated students. Before we knew it, we were talking about the power of love, the joys and difficulties of true neighborliness and the long-haul work of human hopefulness. Who would want to be a hater when it comes to these things? Why not pay this busy little book club a visit from time to time?

It was right about then that he felt understandably compelled to drop a clarifying word amid our escalating love fest: "Nobody doesn't believe in God as much as I do." Boom. Was it something I said? Can we still be friends?

I was pleasantly stumped and strangely excited. Why the rush to disassociate? Was there a problem? Did he think I was trying to sell him on something? I wasn't looking to keep him on any kind of hook or ask him to sign a statement of belief, but I *so* didn't want our commonality to end. I wanted him to know—and said so—that he was kin to many a psalmist, poet and pilgrim *within* the Bible who shared his disbelief. I wanted him to believe that there was still *so much* we could have a good time talking about. Was there a way I might playfully overcome this defensiveness? How might I keep the frequency open?

Here's what I'm up to. I come to you as one bummed out by the way people talk about religion. Be it an online rant, a headline, a news report or a conversation overheard, I feel a jolt of sympathy pain whenever someone characterizes someone else as religious. It's as if a door just got slammed. A person has been somehow shrink-wrapped. Some sweet and perfectly interesting somebody gets left out. And in a subtle, hard-to-get-a-handle-on kind of way, it's kind of like someone's been told to shut up.

This is the way it goes with our words. When I label people, I no longer have to deal with them thoughtfully. I no longer have to feel overwhelmed by their complexity, the lives they live, the dreams they have. I know exactly where they are inside—or forever outside—my field of care, because they've been *taken care of.* The mystery of their existence has been solved and filed away before I've had a chance to be moved by them or even begun to catch a glimpse of who they might be. They've been neutralized. There's hardly any action quite so undemanding, so utterly unimaginative, as the affixing of a label. It's the costliest of mental shortcuts.

Of course we get to call it like we see it. What else can we do? But when we do so with undue haste, when we're neither remotely inquisitive nor especially curious in our regard for other people, we may find that a casual demonization comes to pepper our conversations. This is why it often seems to me that calling someone liberal, conservative, fundamentalist, atheist or extremist is to largely deal in curse words. It puts a person in what we take to be their place, but it only speaks in shorthand. When I go no further in my consideration of my fellow human, I betray my preference for caricature over perception, a shrug as opposed to a vision of the lived fact of somebody in a body. In the face of a perhaps beautifully complicated life, I've opted for oversimplification.

And so it goes with the application of that impossibly broad brush called religion. It's as if we can't even speak the word without walking into the minefield of someone else's wounds. Guards go up immediately and with good reason. It's the ultimate conversation-stopper, an association to end all associations. Who would want to get caught anywhere near it? And in our day, could calling someone religious ever function as a compliment? It's one more label we use as a placeholder of persons and populations, as if we've somehow gotten to the bottom of who they are with an adjective.

I want very much to take this attitude aside and punch it lovingly in the stomach. I want good humor and candor and more truth between us than a label could ever afford. And if it's the case that mention of religion mostly shuts conversation down, I want very badly to somehow crack it open again. If we're open to it, the word need not always signal a dead end; it might even be a means to a breakthrough, a way of fessing up to the facts of what we're all up to.

RELIGION AS CONTROLLING STORY

Let's talk about religion. In its root meaning, religion (from the Latin *religare*, to bind again, to bind back) is simply a tying together, a question of how we see fit to organize ourselves and our resources, a question, we might say, of how things have been tied together so far *and* of how they might be tied together differently, a binding, an unbinding and a binding again. As has always been the case, the organizing of selves and societies can go beautifully or badly or both, but the development of bonds—like the dissolution of bonds—is inescapable. With this in mind, I find it most helpful to define religion as follows: a religion is a controlling story, and there are at least as many as there are people. Stories change but the fact of story doesn't. When we escape a bad story—or see through one into the shock, the awe or the absurdity of what's *really* going on—we haven't escaped stories; we've simply awakened our way into better and truer ones, and we've probably only managed that feat with the considerate assistance of others, whether living or dead. No one awakens all by themselves. Conversions occur all the time. For better *and* worse, we drink the Kool-Aid. Religion happens.

We're often admonished to keep religion out of politics (or vice versa), and civil exchange does require that no one be allowed to hog the microphone while decreeing that the God in his head trumps the reasoning power in everyone else's. But human life won't divide itself up quite so neatly. Given the overwhelming complications of trying to negotiate a just, joyful and more-helpful-than-not existence in a world of raw data with which we often have no idea what to do, we can perhaps be forgiven for wanting to rope off one issue from the other. ("That's political. That's religious. That's a private matter. This is worship. That's a guilty pleasure. And this one over here is just . . . it's just business. It is what it is. It's nothing personal. Sorry about that.") But these divisions can obscure the living fact of certain connections and often leave us estranged from our own sense of ourselves, insulated from the possibility of undivided living.

If we're willing to apply religion to the whole of our own lives as readily as we level it at others, it can wonderfully disrupt whatever it was we thought we were talking about, whatever we thought we had in mind and hand. Like culture, it cuts to the core of what we're really doing and believing, of what values—we all have them—lurk behind our words and actions. Yes, we can use it to disavow and detract. ("I *used* to be religious." "I'm spiritual but not religious." "Let's keep religion out of it.") But I believe there's something dishonest and deluded at work when we speak as if it's only other people who are guided by unreasoning rage or strange notions about the way the world works, only others who, as the saying goes, have an agenda. In this view, *religion* is only a word for the way intellectually underdeveloped people get carried away, a snob's word, and it strikes me as a strange disowning of one's own vulnerability and, if you like, gullibility; it's a rude denial of the fact of our common creatureliness.

My fellow creatures, I propose that we not play that way. If what we believe is what we see is what we do is who we are, there's no getting away from religion. We all want to know who we are, where and how we fit in, and what our lives might yet mean. And in this sense, *religion* might be the best word we have for seeing, naming, confessing and really waking up to what we're after in all we do, of becoming aware of what's going on in our minds. Putting religion on the table in this way, if we're open to doing so, might be the most pressing, interesting and wide-ranging conversation we can have. We might even find ourselves amused.

How's that? Because religion can radically name the specific ways we've put our lives together and, perhaps more urgently, the ways we've allowed other people to put our lives together for us. To be clear, I'm not trying to encourage anyone to begin self-identifying *as* religious. That's as futile and redundant a move as calling yourself political or cultural. But I *am* arguing that we should cease and desist from referring to others as religious as if they're participants in games we ourselves aren't playing, as if they're somehow weirdly and hopelessly enmeshed in cultures of which we're always only detached observers. On the one hand, this is a distancing move that keeps us detached from the fact of our own enthusiasms, our own rituals, our own enmeshments and our own loves. But it also holds another person—the ostensibly religious person—under a scrutiny I have yet to apply to myself. Calling someone else religious doesn't answer the question of my own.

RELIGION AS RELATIONSHIP

To be attentive to the question of religion is to see relationally, to examine the stories we inherit and hand down to others without too much thought as well as those we cobble together to work a crowd, fund a campaign, target a market or convince ourselves to get out of bed in the morning. Sociology invites us to form the words *belief systems* around these phenomena. Doing so is profoundly helpful in the work of achieving a degree of critical distance when it comes to our perceived have-tos. ("Our belief systems may differ here and there, but we both want better public schools, right? *Right.*") And in the age-old task of listening sympathetically to our fellow creatures, of imagining them well, we need all the help we can get. Thank you, social science.

But I'm not sure anyone's ever experienced enlightenment, been born again, been called to repentance or decided to sell their belongings on account of a system. The voice, the tale, the image, the parable that gets through to you—that *wins your heart*—religiously is the one that makes it past your defenses. You've been won over, and you probably didn't see it coming. You've been enlisted into a drama, whether positively or negatively, and it shouldn't be controversial to note that it happens all the time. When you really think about it, there's one waiting around every corner. It's as near as the story, song or image you can't get out of your head.

Religion happens when we get pulled in, moved, called out or compelled by something outside ourselves. It could be a car commercial, a lyric, a painting, a theatrical performance or the magnetic pull of an Apple store. The calls to worship are everywhere. And when we see as much, we begin to understand why Marx would insist that "the critique of religion is the prerequisite of every critique." It is that with which we have to do (or the way we do everything we do or think we do). It is certainly often an opiate for the masses, but it can also function as the poetry of the people. Whether we spy it in ritual, symbol or ceremony, religion isn't something one can be coherently for or against or decide to somehow suddenly engage, because it's always already there. Or as the old Palmolive commercial once put it, we're *soaking* in it.

Whatever the content of the script we're sticking to for dear life—
that would be our religion—it binds us for worse or for better till we
begin to critique it religiously and relentlessly, in view of the possibility of conversion to better boundedness, different and more redeeming orientations or, to put it a little strangely, *less bad* religion.
And a person's religiosity is never not in play. It names the patterns,
shifting or consistent, avowed or not, of all our interactions. Religion
is the question of how we dispose our energies, how we see fit to
organize our own lives and, in many cases, the lives of others.

This need be neither buzzkill nor bummer. On the contrary, it's an
invitation to be more present to my own life, to access and examine
more deeply what I'm up to. It also levels the playing field more than
a little, because suddenly a Muslim going to prayers isn't more or less
religious than a grown man with a big piece of pretend cheese on his
head going to watch a Green Bay Packers game. Is it good religion?
Bad religion? True? False? Idolatrous? Righteous? Opinions will vary.
But to hit Pause long enough to consider *the content* of our devotion,
our lives and our investments is to begin to see the question clearly.
What are my controlling stories? Do I like the stories my one life tells?
Do I need to see about changing them?

In this sense, we're never *not* speaking and acting upon our religion. We're never *not* involved in everyday worship. We're always
in the thick of it, this living fact of what our human hands have
wrought under the dictation of what's actually going on in our
human hearts and minds. Our real sense of what's really sacred is
regularly on display. David Byrne of the Talking Heads bears
witness to the religious situation when he invites us to consider the
cities. Having made a regular habit of biking through as many as he
can as often as he can, he describes his ongoing realization that
cities are nothing less than "physical manifestations of our deepest
beliefs and our often unconscious thoughts." It's merely a matter of
recognition: "A cognitive scientist need only look at what we have

made—the hives we have created—to know what we think and what we believe to be important. . . . It's all there, in plain view, right out in the open." We evade. We compartmentalize. We say *this* doesn't have anything to do with *that*. But what we're up to isn't, as it turns out, a secret: "You don't need CAT scans and cultural anthropologists to show you what's going on inside the human mind; its inner workings are manifested in three dimensions." Our religion, practically speaking, is, after all, alarmingly self-evident if we're open to taking a hard look around: "Our values and hopes are sometimes awfully embarrassingly easy to read. They're right there—in the storefronts, museums, temples, shops, and office buildings. . . . They say, in their unique visual language, 'This is what we think matters, this is how we live and how we play.'"[1]

No Communion Without Nuance

Like God and the devil, religion is in the details. Like any artist, Byrne would have us begin to think about them, to lean into the fact of certain connections we're in the weird habit of denying, to move through the world with our antennae out, saying—or singing— what we see. To do so artfully is to engage in the kind of poetic thinking we associate with Byrne or any creative personality determined to be awake and alive to the myths in which we otherwise swim unknowingly, myths in which we've been immersed so long that they've become second nature to us, myths by and through which we've measured our lives so unconsciously that we've forgotten how arbitrary they are, myths from which we're perfectly free to withdraw our consent when we begin to ask ourselves, "Well, how did we get here?"

To genuinely ask this kind of question is to be a practitioner of simple self-awareness, a way of wondering at ourselves and all the strange things we put up with, sustain and perpetuate, a way of bringing it all to consciousness. What task could be more urgent for a person? For my money, religion is the farthest-reaching readily available concept for looking hard and honestly at our own lives, for *really* leveling with ourselves and for abandoning our dysfunctional ideas for better ones, truer, livelier, more sustainable ways of negotiating our existence. Life's too short to pretend we're not religious.

Why do I insist on framing the conversation this way? I'm in it for beauty. As someone who has dared to try to teach people for most of my adult life, I often suspect that what I'm up to is, in large part, an effort to try to stop people from becoming bored and giving up too soon, to help them find their own lives and the lives of others powerfully interesting, weird and somehow beautiful. Look again, *re*-spect, stay with me and consider the possibility that there might be more going on in a neighbor, a novel, an image or an issue than your mind grasped the first time around, something worthy of your time, something beautiful. In this, I share Elaine Scarry's conviction that the "willingness continually to revise one's own location in order to place oneself in the path of beauty is the basic impulse underlying education."[2] This is to define education as a journey, certainly, but it is also to envision education as a creative task that involves finding and seeing beauty in the very places where we've grown accustomed to only sensing and feeling conflict.

Which brings us back to religion as a divider. I want very badly to challenge the ease with which we succumb to the false divide of labels, that moment in which our empathy gives out and we refuse to respond openhandedly or even curiously to people with whom we differ. As I see it, to refuse the possibility of finding another person interesting, complex and as complicated as oneself is a form of violence. At bottom, this is a refusal of nuance, and I wish to posit that nuance is sacred. To call it sacred is to value it so much and esteem it so highly that we find it fitting to somehow set it apart as something to which we're forever committed. Nuance refuses to envision others degradingly, denying them the content of their own experience, and talks us down tenderly from the false ledges we've put ourselves on. When we take it on as a sacred obligation, nuance also delivers us out of the deadly habit of cutting people out of our own imaginations. This opens us up to the possibility of at least occasionally finding one another beautiful, the possibility of communion. I happen to live for these openings, and I suspect I write "NUANCE" in the margins of research papers more than any other word. It could be that there's no communion without it.

I hasten to add that the communion I'm hoping for isn't a retreat from the everyday or the realistic but a more profound engagement with it. This brings to mind Iris Murdoch's definition of love: "Love is the extremely difficult realisation that something other than oneself is real. Love, and so art and morals, is the discovery of reality."[3]

The work of consciousness, we begin to understand, is never done.

RELIGION IS WITNESS

In this vein, I offer my vision of religion as central to all human experience as a way of getting unstuck from our failures of imagination in the way we see ourselves and others, those mean mental habits with which we casually but all too definitively deny commitment, connection and kinship to neighbors, strangers and family when they disturb our defensive sense of our own identities. By letting religion name all our own ultimate concerns and the ways we pursue them, we open our lives to an ever-renewed perception and recognition of our profoundly interdependent relationship to the rest of the world. I view this as a summons to see ourselves anew *and* to discover reality as it is—not *making* connections exactly, because the truth is they're already there, preceding us as the very facts on the ground, whether we recognize them or not. To begin to respond to such a summons is to enter the kind of accountability—the deep awareness—that occurs when we see and think poetically, because poetry is the work of recognition, the work of seeing beautifully.

It would have been a mouthful, and good conversations know no definitive ending, but what I hoped to convey—and still do—to my disbelieving friend is that we lose no ground when we note that there are myriad ways to be a true believer and that we might even gain something in the way of candor, ownership, transparency and substance if we can fess up to our own devotions. What manner of devotee art thou? What's the what, the how and the why of your day-to-day? Let's hold our devotions out with open hands. Or as Leonard Cohen so memorably puts it, let us compare mythologies.

It's a life's work for sure, but with humor and compassion we can try to own what we're up to; we can try to be true in all we do. Your obsession with *Game of Thrones*? Religious. Your determination to hold on to that plastic bottle till you've found a recycling receptacle? Religious. The song you sing when you're alone? Religious. Your response to your fellow pilgrim who just cut you off in traffic? Religious. The bad ideas you're leaving behind *and* the new ones you're trying on: Religious.

You're always telling your controlling story. Or to borrow a phrase from Jesus of Nazareth, we'll be known by our fruit. The operative term—the excruciatingly helpful word I have in mind here—is witness. As much as I'd often prefer otherwise, there is no on-and-off switch when it comes to my witness. It's simply the evidence of my output. My witness is the sum of everything I do and leave undone. The words are there, but the actions speak louder.

Our witness isn't what we say we believe or even what we think we believe. Neither is it the image, pose or posture we try to present to others. It's what we do, what we give, what we take and what we actually bring to our little worlds. Witness knows no division. In some sense, the future will know what our witness was better than we can, the ways we rang true (or didn't). Time's the revelator when it comes to what your witness is or what your religion, as it turns out, was. Your religion is your witness is the shape your love takes. In all things.

But I'm getting ahead of myself. Before I go too far asking anyone to consider the ups and downs of their weird religious background, I'd like to devote some space to describing, as best as I can, my own. For every hero or villain, there's always an origin story. Here's hoping that our neuroses might also be, in some deep sense, our wisdom. I'll go first.

1

Crackers and grape juice

People who can't make the world into a story, go mad.

Ursula K. Le Guin

PICTURE AN EIGHTIES ERA SEVENTEEN-YEAR-OLD in horn-rimmed glasses and a maroon vest sitting in a box office waiting for a late-night movie audience to appear. It could have been *The Princess Bride or Top Gun* or *No Way Out*. The responsibility that befell me was to sell tickets, eat popcorn and talk to customers about the only thing I really wanted to talk about anyway. I asked strangers what their favorite movies were to help them come to a decision, and they'd thank me for sharing my expertise. Conversations never ended quite so beautifully among my peers, but here, I'd found my people.

But on this particular evening I'd forgotten something. I knew it was a Sunday and felt bad about having *labored* on that day. I had an image of my grandfather, a lifelong farmer, reading his newspaper in a rocking chair, attired in his Sunday best till the sun went down and it seemed permissible to feed the mules. But it wasn't too long since we'd enjoyed an episode of the *Dukes of Hazzard* together. All was well between us, and the working-on-a-Sunday business was not a big problem. This was something else.

At about a quarter to midnight I suddenly realized I was staring down the barrel of having missed, for the first Sunday since my baptism, taking Communion, what we called the Lord's Supper, and this was decidedly *not* okay. Nobody had spelled out such quandaries to me explicitly, but in my head such negligence could potentially constitute a kind of cosmic deal breaker. Baptism, as I understood it, was a one-time deal, and there would be no further cleansing water to erase this particular stain of negligence. There was the lurking feeling that, this time around, my scarlet-stained soul would *not* be rendered white as snow, and, try as I might, I couldn't get it out of my mind. Feigning calm, I asked a coworker to mind the shop and made for the door.

If you had been in Nashville at a nearby Kroger in 1987, you might have witnessed an anxious, wing-tipped young man running up and down the aisles searching desperately for saltine crackers and Welch's grape juice. Once past the register, I made my way briskly toward the exit and paused in the parking lot to say a quick prayer to the God who, as far as I could tell, appeared to demand these things. I stared at the starry sky above as I wolfed down the crackers and juice with seconds remaining and laughed to myself. I'd made it . . . for now.

Do you find this ridiculous? Pitiful? Horribly sad? I'd like to say that I do, too, even as I still feel deep kinship with this confused young person. His ability to find *himself* ridiculous and to laugh at his own thinking saves the scene, in my view, and renders the situation a little less tragic. When I wonder how a crazed fundamentalist could laugh at himself, I find myself back at the movie theater, that bastion of story and song where so many an epiphany has come to me my whole life long. I wasn't, strictly speaking, alone in that parking lot. I couldn't help but wonder, for instance, what Steve Martin might make of my passionate performance. And as earnest and afraid as I was, I certainly couldn't deny that my trembling ingestion of juice and crackers would fit perfectly in an episode of my beloved *Twilight Zone*. And were the crew of the starship *Enterprise* to stumble upon an individual on some lonely planet where getting the timing right on such a ritual was ascribed such earth-shattering significance, it seemed to me that Captain Kirk might think it needful, one more time, to go ahead and violate the Prime Directive for me, for mercy's sake. My bemused laughter, you begin to understand, arose from a certain not-at-all-aloneness I owed to a great cloud of pop-culture witnesses surrounding me and affording me more than a few fragments to shore up against my psychological ruin. How might we best characterize the impact of such influences on my troubled mind? Before I attempt to answer this question, I'd like to share a related story.

Spot the Sensitive One

A month or two later, I made my way to a friend's eighteenth birthday party. His parents were divorced, and the celebration was at his father's place. It was a guys-only affair.

We all stood around the kitchen talking about being seniors and applying to colleges while going to work on Doritos and soft drinks. There was a giggle every so often about a special surprise in store for us that evening, and the few who appeared to be in the know would exchange wide-eyed looks before changing the subject to add to the suspense. My friend's father would smile and shake his head. In time there came a knock at the door. It was opened to reveal a woman in a trench coat, I think, smiling.

Thanks to a senior English project, I'd been reading Dostoevsky novels all year and was lately in the habit of concluding that I alone, like some sensitive Russian monk, could be expected to hold to the standard of genuine humanness in scenes of tragic degradation. Add to this a certain sanctimoniousness, and you can imagine how bewildered and blindsided I felt at the nearness of an affable woman completely bare but for strategically placed tassels required by Tennessee state law. As perfunctory cheers, whistles and the forced laughter of my peers anxiously filled every second of awkward silence, I politely declined the offer to place a five-dollar bill between hip and elastic and negotiated a timely exit.

Feeling more than a little estranged from my friends and that I might have failed them in some way, I turned on the tape deck in my mother's Caprice Classic and was greeted by the weird and welcome world of a treasured Tom Waits cassette. To be clear, barreling down the interstate listening to "Hang On St. Christopher" off *Franks Wild Years* did not render the universe or my role within it any less problematic, but it did have me feeling less left out of things and even a tiny bit vindicated. According to my antagonized imagination, a raspy-voiced, world-weary, imaginative man like Waits represented certain otherwise unavailable sympathies. It was as if he'd forgotten more than my rowdy friends would ever know, and he was on *my* side—worried over the kinds of things that worried me and alive to certain contradictions and hypocrisies I was also determined to be alive to.

Perhaps this is the way it works for many of us. At the risk of sounding obsessive, I suspect I'm like a lot of people for whom music is *anything but* a distraction, a little something to take my mind off things. I wasn't simply amused or entertained by Tom Waits. I was and I am, in no small way, devoted to him. He had me at the raspy "Hello" of a music video in which he came at me as a bleary, strangely contented homeless man in a prop room singing to a mannequin through a bullhorn. I felt beckoned to see my own life and the lives of others differently, called out to see what he's showing, the strange, sideways view of reality he posits, a view in which everything is weirdly connected to everything else. Waits is in the showing business after all, right? I find him completely and utterly convincing. He helps me to *get real*.

THIS HAS TO DO WITH THAT

This brings me back to Steve Martin and Rod Serling's *The Twilight Zone* and how they arose in the mind of the nervy young fellow trying to avert God's wrath in a Kroger parking lot. We have, on the one hand, a teenage lifetime of sermons and Sunday school curriculums, my own lonely grappling with Scripture, and all the weird fears I figured were backed up in the Bible somewhere. And on the other, there was a hodgepodge of reading, listening, television viewing, stories, *Saturday Night Live* and *SCTV* skits, stand-up routines and pop-culture songs through which my friends and I tried to make sense of ourselves and find patterns to live by. I dwelt, like everyone does, in the tension between what I was into and what I was supposed to be into.

But mercifully, in my view, I never bought into the notion that these experiences belonged in different hands or that I was somehow dealing with competing truths between which I had to make an adult decision, and soon. I couldn't quite draw that kind of line anyway, given the fact, for instance, that I remember the day of my baptism mostly because *Superman II* aired on ABC that night. I had yet to hear of a secular and sacred divide but, then as now, it dissolved upon contact with the way my heart works. To isolate one from the other is to tidy up matters a little too untruthfully, cordoning off "the religious" from "the worldly" in a manner that doesn't ring true to my experience or, I suspect, anyone else's.

I had—and have—before me a wide array of references to regulate my inner dramas, whether a poem, a scene in a Stanley Kubrick film, a relative in a rocking chair, a Bible verse or an episode of *Doctor Who*. I have many strands with which to build and rebuild my web of meaning—I do it without thinking about it—and many means to reconnect when disconnection occurs. Many advocates, real and imagined, beckon me back when I suspect I've decisively strayed from sane society.

Consider again the grape juice and crackers in my trembling hands and my desperate hold on what I thought might prove to be a cosmically costly loose end. I didn't want to live in a world where, in a moment like that, my enthusiasms weren't allowed to address me, as if my crisis was so narrowly religious that it somehow sealed me off from the rest of the human world and all its saving associations. I badly needed to overcome this artificial divide. I still do. I have to let one voice speak to another by way of rebuke, correction or affirmation. I want a wide-open world made new, again and again, by bigger and better pictures of who I am and what I might yet be. Perhaps this is an interest common to everyone.

To affirm that a film or a comic book has been a means of grace to me is to begin to take stock of my own multitude of counselors, the voices I depend upon to make better and more artful sense of myself and others. Why not see what all's in there? Why not hold it out with open hands?

COMMON HUMAN CULTURE

When we think of our available means for regaining balance, restoring lost continuities or reconstituting a sense of reality, we're in the thick of the deepest meaning of what we've come to call religion. Recall again that religion *is* rebinding, that tying together of the ties that bind us, whether for good or ill. And the question of religion is the question of who and what we're bound to, how it is we find ourselves tied up and what our biggest big ideas actually are, the ideas to which we find ourselves helplessly,

> **The question of religion is the question of who and what we're bound to, how it is we find ourselves tied up and what our biggest big ideas actually are.**

unknowingly or even gratefully attached. Whether we have in mind a highlight or a hang-up, a recurrent anxiety or an ecstatic epiphany, religion names our social bonds, and, needless to say, we all have them.

Understandably, there are very solid reasons for resisting such a broad conception of what religion means. Many among us feel so damaged by the psychological trauma of our upbringing, so embarrassed by the strange and outrageous things we only recently believed so fervently, that the word serves wonderfully well for drawing a line between brainwash and rational thought. *I'm not religious* signals firmly that I'm not falling for that backward madness anymore, and I won't be made to sit quietly when someone starts singing that sad, confusing song. It also conjures a little distance between cool reason and the crazies. Spiritual? Sure. But religious? You refer of course to those awkward people who only speak in monologue, right? What's to be done with folks with the unfortunate habit of mistaking the voice of God for the voice in their heads and acting accordingly? We know too well how it goes when they hold political office, sit on school boards or acquire combustible materials. They destroy our hopes for an otherwise sensibly secular scene in which people are people, appeals to reason aren't punished and nobody plays the God card. Why ruin any- and everything with religion? Isn't coming out of it alive what evolution is for?

Believe me, I get it. And if we lived in a world in which this is all the word *religion* was allowed to mean, I'd certainly line up with those fighting against it. After all, nobody wants to get caught advocating for militant ignorance. But what good is the word if we only use it to describe the foolishness of others? If we mean for religion to encapsulate *all* allegedly sacred visions, *every* designation of the holy and *anything* that's ever passed for a wisdom tradition, we could be dealing with an inconceivably large target. Religion, in this sense, is a concept too general to be meaningfully *for* and too abstract to be coherently *against.* Taking a stand *against* religion is no more sensible that being opposed to promises, the forming of a line at Starbucks or the power of association. Being *for* it is as strange a conviction as delighting in mobs, mass hysteria or assemblies. To really believe we can successfully undertake either is to be stunningly inattentive to the wonderfully complicated offerings of our common human culture.

Perhaps there's a less radioactive way of talking about these things. Until we get to the actual content of someone's allegedly religious activity (volunteering in a soup kitchen, executing an adulterer, fasting for immigration reform, burning a flag or physically attacking someone who's decided to do so), religion is no more necessarily harmful or harmless than, say, an angle of vision. Neil Gaiman offers a helpful word in this regard: "Religions are places to stand and look and act, vantage points from which to view the world."[1] But even if we're all situated—seeing, speaking and acting from and within a particular vantage point—there has to be a certain fluidity at play. When it comes to traditions, for instance— and there is no religion without them—they're always changing, dying and coming back to life.

Tradition (derived from the Latin *tradere*, to transfer) is simply that which has passed down the pipeline, the stories and images we only truly inherit through redeployment. Old ceremonies are practiced anew in unforeseen contexts, taking on fresh new meaning. The life of traditions *is* their mobility. They're handed down, passed around, borrowed from and mulled upon. They're as varied and divided as their supposed adherents. In this sense, religions are so dynamic and in process that we can't nail one down or, as much as we'd like to think we could, somehow analyze one definitively. You can't step in the same religion twice.

As a young fellow trying to perform a religious ceremony in a parking lot, I was in desperate need of a little mobility, a more fluid take on my own religious situation than I'd had up until then (be baptized and consume crackers and juice with due reverence on the first day of each week, and you'll probably escape eternal torment). Somehow—and I know it doesn't go this way for everyone—I knew that I need not be all hemmed in alone, stuck, afraid and isolated with my debilitating ideas about God and eternity. My vantage point remained blessedly susceptible or porous enough to admit the influence of other voices, other vantage points that came to my aid to help me find myself funny, weird and not entirely alone. You can guess the mess I would have been in if someone had persuaded me I wasn't allowed to read, see and take in whatever struck me as interesting.

HUNTING AND GATHERING

Having felt free—and even called—to dabble widely, it would be difficult to think, as many do, of my religious background as a crime that was enacted against me, but I imagine I would if it had been reduced to a narrow sliver of Christianity, only meaning what I took it to mean in my especially confused moments as a teenager. In my struggle to make sense of myself and to distinguish between what's real and what's not, my vision of Christianity doesn't center around anxiety concerning the afterlife; it's also the freshening flow of a tradition fluid and alive enough to mean more than what I had reduced it to. And in my case, placing Tom Waits and the world of cinema to the side of my religious formation won't do justice to the gift of awareness they give me. To speak of either as a side issue is to distort the fact of the situation. Surely everybody's consciousness is more complicated than our careless tendency to confine and categorize will allow. Why keep the poetic and the prophetic unartfully separated from one another? The stories and songs that give us life, that render us more attentive to the lives we're living—what are they if not religious?

"People who can't make the world into a story, go mad," novelist

Ursula K. Le Guin observed. And I suppose there's a sense in which I'm always on a pilgrimage of hunting and gathering whatever I can find that might help me cobble together a more inspiringly coherent account of my own experience, reaching for anything, really, that might somehow illumine my darkness. As a young boy, this took the form of a devotion to the Incredible Hulk, King Kong and probably any strong, misunderstood creature whose displacement led to the destruction of property. I am one who, as a child, once labored on a vivid, colorful and detailed picture of Godzilla with his name emblazoned in large capital letters, presented it humbly to his grandmother and had it handed back immediately with the decree: "There's only one God." Message received. *That* can't have anything to do with *this*. Getting out from under it takes some doing.

I imagine these mean little dichotomies being dropped on children young and old the world over, and I hope to bring an end to them whenever I can. I come by my determined, lifelong refusal of these divisions honestly. If undivided vision goes, then meaning, coherence and a loving future go with it. It's a matter of personal sanity. I want everything connected to everything else, a sacred whole. Spot the weird religious background.

But of course the casual squashing of a child's living imagination isn't the sum total of the peculiar inheritance vouchsafed unto me. There

> **I want everything connected to everything else, a sacred whole.**

were also many matters of conscience that got instilled—mostly blessedly, I'd say—early on. The grandmother of whom I speak would correct me if, upon parting, I presumed aloud I'd see her again come Christmas. *"If the Lord wills*, we will see each other again," she would intone in macabre fashion with raised eyebrows. And this is perhaps incontestably the handing down of a hang-up, but, for my part, I wouldn't be quick to trade it away, even as I'm careful to avoid passing these obsessions over wholesale to my children.

WISDOM AND NEUROSIS

A religious background, whatever form it takes, is a mixed bag. My grandmother's often domineering determination never to speak or allow an idle word had at least a root or two in those ancient communal efforts toward wholeness and healing we call sacred traditions. Let your "yes" mean yes and your "no" mean no, and anything extra—a vow, for instance—is likely manipulative filler or perhaps a toxic denial of your own finitude, a claim to know more than you can personally guarantee. Perhaps this is a tradition worthy of maintaining: say what you mean. And if we define tradition, bad or good, as that which has been handed down to us, it might simply name the ongoing process whereby we parse out what we've inherited: the true, the real and the life giving, or the dysfunctional, degrading and death dealing. Traditions are everywhere. Throw a rock and you'll hit one.

When it comes to this particular Dark family tradition of watching one's language, I confess I have a similar relationship with the idle word. Say I'm late to class and, in an attempt at humor, I apologize and say I had to snap the neck of an assassin, or that parking was complicated by the fact that I rode into work on a Ferris wheel. Even when I know my students know I'm just goofing around, I feel obliged to whisper almost inaudibly, "Just kidding." It's as if I can't release an untruth into the air without feeling the need to swat it down somehow.

Is this habit only a centimeter away from the young lunatic in the parking lot? Perhaps so, but it's my inheritance, and I'm trying to make the most of it. I suspect it can be a salubrious quirk as well as a source of paranoia and entertainment. As much as it complicates things, trying very hard not to lie isn't a bad way to live. This might be a legacy fit to hold on to. Either way, there it sits. As ever, our neuroses and our wisdom are closely aligned.

PLEASE OPEN YOUR BIBLES

This is also the case in my lifelong relationship of love and fear, assurance and anxiety, when it comes to the Bible. I used to worry about placing other books on top of it lest it appear to have been marginalized in my presence. I'd read it all the way through—or at least make sure my eyes passed over each word—at a very early age for fear of what might become of me if I got caught dead without having done so. Better safe than sorry, my logic went. The same reasoning was applied in the mental gymnastics I carried out in an effort to assure myself and others that the entire thing was void of contradiction.

For example, at the age of sixteen I preached a sermon that hinged on the scene in Luke's Gospel where a dying thief crucified beside Jesus asks to be remembered by him when he enters his kingdom. Jesus tells him, "Today you will be with me in Paradise." A moving exchange in itself, I could acknowledge, but in my need to know that the Bible was consistent and that everything within it added up appropriately into one unified doctrine, this extension of a saving word to a thief about whom we knew almost nothing constituted a bit of a problem. What to do?

It's all very simple, I explained. Because the Bible is without contradiction, we can infer that this thief was probably among the multitude baptized by John the Baptist and can safely assume that Jesus, either through omniscience or a kind of built-in baptism scanner, was capable of knowing as much as he gazed upon him. Otherwise, he would have known not to say such a thing. Problem solved. Any questions?

It's embarrassing—but instructive—to note that this is the troubled spot where I've lived a sizable chunk of my life. I hasten to add, however, that it's largely where I remain. If I'm blessed with a long enough life, I hope and pray that I'll look back with fondness on my forty-five-year-old, well-intentioned, Bible-reading self. I'd like to think I don't cling to my own interpretations quite so nervously and defensively, but who's to say?

There was a time when I was suspicious of commentary and footnotes, as if they were a grossly human hindrance to God's direct communication with the reader, but I think of them now as a crucial means to not reading it badly or even murderously, of reading it well and carefully and alive to context. I thank God for footnotes. And as long as everyone's allowed to speak, I've yet to meet a Bible study group I didn't like.

Somewhere back there, I was shown that the Bible, as a collection of very different texts canonized as Scripture over time, should never be read flatly, as if a decree to slay Edomites in one verse, for instance, can be rightly used to counter the prophetic call to provide for a foreigner or to love an enemy in another. Or as if there is no movement, development or ethical evolution within the collection itself. The biblical tradition, to which I try to remain true, contains traditions within itself that appeal to one another, counter one another and sometimes leave one another behind. ("You have heard that it was said, but I say to you . . ." "Do not remember the things of old . . .") Weirdly enough, committing myself to it, in spirit and in truth, means to hold fast to movement, to receptivity, to new and unforeseen goodness on the horizon, to what the Spirit of the Lord might be saying to us in our contemporary context.

IS IT RIGHT FOR YOU TO BE ANGRY?

As I understand it, the biblical tradition chronicles *its own* movement through the kinds of texts its Scripture-collecting communities decreed somehow essential, even when they had plenty of good reasons for finding them embarrassing. When I say that I believe this process and the texts it yields to be inspired, I mean to express my delight and amazement at the inclusion, for instance, of a book like Jonah, famously a deal breaker for many readers given the bit about the man chilling out in the belly of a big fish for three days. I'm a fan for other reasons.

With four short chapters, this tale—named for its angry and confused prophet-protagonist—can be read in under five minutes. We don't find out why until the end, but upon receiving word from on high that he is to go east to Nineveh, capital of Assyria, to announce God's anger against the wickedness of its population, Jonah immediately goes west to board a boat and flee these instructions. As the story goes, God hurls a wind upon the sea to get Jonah off the ship whose polytheistic crew clearly fear and worship God with more reverence than he does. When they reluctantly deposit him overboard, God commissions the oversized fish to gingerly engulf the prophet and spew him forth on a beach three days later.

Things get weirder. He now journeys to and prophesies against Nineveh concerning its God-ordained destruction within forty days. With no assurance that doing so will win them a reprieve, the Ninevites undertake a mass action of city-wide repentance with everyone, from the king to the people to—very strangely—the animals, fasting and donning sackcloth. The cartoonish, extreme lengths to which Nineveh goes in response to the Jewish prophet's word of judgment would be especially shocking for the story's original audience, for whom Assyrians were held in general contempt. In any case, the God Annihilates Nineveh Tour is canceled.

Here we discover why Jonah earlier fled from the Lord, and it wasn't because he didn't like dissing the Ninevites. On the contrary, it was because he knew that God had a way of flipping the prophetic script once Jonah had voiced it. Yet again, the people with a long biblical history of being the objects of God's rage are suddenly beloved of God and no longer beyond the cultural pale. God isn't angry, but Jonah is. He falls into a recurrent depression over this familiar pattern of moving goalposts. Jonah tells people, in God's name, that they're gonna get it, only to watch God go soft. As in the beginning of the story, he would rather die than keep being a means of God's goodness to wicked Gentiles.

"Is it right for you to be angry?" God asks Jonah as the latter takes a seat outside the city to observe the promised destruction he now knows will never come. And the object lesson we've seen underway from the beginning continues. God appoints a bush to arise from the ground and provide Jonah with shade, to be followed at sunup by a worm who dutifully destroys the bush, depriving Jonah of relief. God prepares a sultry wind that has Jonah languishing to the point of asking that he might be permitted to die.

"Is it right for you to be angry about the bush?" God asks.

"Angry enough to die," Jonah assures him. And with a bit of rhetoric that concludes the book—we don't hear from Jonah again— God notes that if Jonah is so attached to something as short-lived as a bush, it's at least arguably permissible for God to have a degree of affection for the people of Nineveh and its livestock. Would that be all right with you, Jonah? Too upsetting? Hmm? Might the prophet enlarge his sympathies a little to include, say, other non-Jewish human beings?

If the divinely appointed worm or the animals in sackcloth aren't enough, the satiric skewering of Jonah on the subject of his own prejudice—and that of many within the Hebrew community that was the story's earliest audience—should show us that what we have here is essentially a *South Park* episode smack-dab in the middle of the Bible. As a lampooning of what is even now a prevalent disposition of many a God-talker, it chronicles a revolutionary realization on the part of its authors concerning who's in and who's out. We can imagine that it probably didn't go over very well initially, as it's doubtless a minority position that celebrates God's lively refusal to be consistent, a refusal to be against the very people that tradition said God would be against forever and ever. Jonah, after all, is prepared to die on the sword of all the things God was supposed to be.

But the tradition moved. And the shift, given its inclusion within the collection that came to be called God's Word, is preserved. In this, the short, satiric folktale hits its target, namely those who might be made to see their own reflection in a man who comically clings to a beloved bush while resisting the call from on high to value an entire beloved world of people and animals, a man suicidal over how his concept *of God* is being destroyed *by God* yet again. By making fun of a certain racist sensibility all too often at work among its own, the community decrees that sweet little Jonah and his ilk are silly, charming and tragically mistaken. The old insistence concerning the boundaries of God's blessing is being dissolved once more.

Does it hit its target now? That depends. If we insist the primary takeaway of the book of Jonah is the need to read every last strange detail (divinely directed fish, bush, worm, winds, etc.) as literal accounts of history, I believe we have yet to see what's going on. Worse, I believe we've perversely traded the sacred-comic insight of the tale for something less intelligible. One can avoid the moral weight of the Bible by only reading it outlandishly. This move occurs among its alleged lovers *and* despisers. In both cases, I think it's a little like saying you tried to love the Harry Potter books until you researched their claims and discovered that Hogwarts doesn't really exist.

THE BIBLE TELLS ME SO

When I say I find the Bible inspired, living, active, sharp as any two-edged sword, amazing in the way that it cuts to the heart of all kinds of unexpected issues and invites us to pay attention to ourselves anew, I don't have in mind a single method for reading it in all times and places and seasons of life. I merely speak as a lifelong enthusiast whose sense of curiosity and wonder at the thing deepens with every reading. I find it remarkable and revolutionary that the Jewish community preserved a tale of God's tenderness toward its own enemies alongside prayers for its enemies' painful deaths. When I contemplate the Bible as it comes down to me, it's as if contrary hopes, lines of reasoning, complaints, letters, gospels, lamentations, dream visions and histories were all squeezed into one space to see what they might produce when taken together, what each might say to the other, what wonderful and unforeseen things might yet come from the mix.

Because it's an ongoing movement, a story without an ending, trying to be true to something like the Bible is the multifaceted work of generations, a communal labor of many lifetimes. For this reason, to presume to have arrived at the right reading to which anyone else who comes to it will have to submit is to go completely bonkers and miss the boat entirely. Like Shakespeare, its life is in being received and reenvisioned again and again, differently and better and truer. And if the latest listening doesn't challenge to some degree whatever it is I had in mind previously, I have yet to pay adequate attention.

Needless to say, my account of the ways in which the Bible operates in my existence is not a tale of how we touched and went our separate ways. I'm still trying to get it right, but doing so doesn't mean clinging to it quite so nervously or exclusively as I once did.

The same goes for a defensive posture toward my own identity. Am I true to the Bible? A Bible believer? I want to be one who is down in its groove, who received and sought to answer the summons to moral seriousness issued by it. But this would have to be the verdict of others—a community, for instance, or anyone who might observe my behavior and speech and discern a certain process at work, a lived commitment. To make that call for myself is, to my mind, no more appropriate than asserting that I've at last achieved enlightenment, orthodoxy or righteousness.

ON THE POSSIBILITY OF BECOMING CHRISTIAN

Whether proffered in an op-ed, in a political campaign or around the dinner table, it seems to me that a sentence that begins with the words "As a Christian . . ." will usually end badly. What do we hope to gain by speaking this way? If we have in mind, say, a lived pursuit of the ethical path taught and exemplified by Jesus of Nazareth, it's a wonderful adjective that can be rightly—and perhaps right-eously—applied to all manner of behavior among all manner of human beings. It's an aspiration of my own, certainly, but to risk deploying it as a self-descriptor is a little tacky. That would be to use the word in vain, to boast at being an obvious bearer of a wisdom I perhaps have yet to deeply receive into my own life. To presume one's own Christianity in this way, as a mission accomplished, is to place the cart before the horse. In this I'm informed by a sensibility I once heard articulated by Maya Angelou who thought it most fitting to speak in terms of repeated attempts and lifelong practice: "I'm grateful to be a practicing Christian. I'm always amazed when people say, 'I'm a Christian.' I think, 'Already?' It's an ongoing process. You know, you keep trying. And blowing it and trying and blowing it."[2] Seeking to live up to this wise take on self-identity, I hesitate to call myself a Christian convert, *unless* I can be understood to mean that I'm not yet done converting to— and learning again what it might mean to convert to—this amazing movement, this centuries-long experiment in humanness some-times referred to as Christianity.

The long-haul work of conversion, we understand, can't be un-dertaken alone. And for me, there are people, a communion of the living and the dead, by whom I'm regularly schooled, nurtured and renewed. They're not all "Christian" in the broadcast-media, self-proclaimed sound-bite sense, but they do constitute a certain witness that hungers and thirsts for a better-ordered world, an assemblage of folks determined to live lives of social righteousness (not that there's any such thing as a righteousness that *isn't* social). I find these people just about everywhere.

And as I experience it, that communion is getting bigger all the time, but the local one, with whom I meet weekly, is a rather small, ragtag congregation of Presbyterians of which I'm pleased to be counted a member. As far as I can tell, I've been largely delivered from the corrosive anxiety that had me ravenously devouring crackers and grape juice in a parking lot, but I'm still eager to dwell along the same trajectory I discerned so dimly as a teenager, even to celebrate it with others in a communal pursuit of all things true and beautiful.

In the historical landmark that generally houses this congregation, there are those who, by their own admission, are only there to feed homeless people; artists who utilize the space and admire their community's ethic but verbally confess few or none of its creeds; and people who are pleased to have a safe place to discuss and disagree agreeably about the Bible. I'm pleased to be there as one more pilgrim struggling with the mix of resources that makes up my heritage—that would be my weird religious background—and the blessing and burden of consciousness and conscience it imposes upon me. It should be obvious by now that I can't imagine leaving it behind but hope instead to consciously confront it, to occasionally define myself against it and to dwell faithfully within it. There are, after all, so many ways to be true to a story, so many ways to be religious.

One of the most visible forms this journey takes is my attention collection. I've already recounted how I've drawn on it in parking lots and interstates. It grows and it changes and it's accompanied me my whole life long, helping to humanize the reality in front of me as I try to see clearly and to somehow feel more at home in my own skin. And it seems obvious to me that we all have one.

What exactly and precisely *is* an attention collection? I'm so glad you asked.

2

Attention collection

Art happens in an act of attention.

Guy Davenport

ONCE WATCHED THE VETERAN SINGER-SONGWRITER Peter Case lead a discussion among young aspiring musicians concerning lifelong habits of creativity. He talked about how the artist operates as a thieving magpie, always on the lookout for bits, threads and fragments that might serve in the assembling of a nest. With the same working survival instinct, the artist draws inspiration from a half-remembered remark, a billboard, an odd facial expression misperceived, a snatch of dialogue among strangers or whatever's at hand—sometimes directly or word-for-word—to articulate something needful, new and timely whether in lyric, image, story or argument.

"How old are you guys?" he asked when a lull had set in. Most reported themselves to be in their late teens and early twenties. Nodding, he surprised everyone by saying, "You've seen enough then. You have more than enough material to get you where you're going." After a pause, "But maybe you haven't *seen* what you've seen."

> **Maybe you haven't *seen* what you've seen.**

What a line. And like a good magpie, I went ahead and made that one my own, repeating it as often as possible, the better to take the admonition to heart and broadcast the call to fuller consciousness whenever occasions permit. And what an essential burden to make sure you're still taking on this business of being awake to yourself—to be a witness to your own experience, to listen to your own life, to see what you've seen. Art is how we become aware of ourselves, and it's *for* everyone. What could be more socially essential, more sacred? After all, nobody can do the work of being true for you.

I come from a long line of teachers. Both my mother and father gave it a go for decades, and the same goes for my sister, brother, aunts, uncles and grandparents. I can't quite mention my own involvement in education without recalling—it's the background speaking again—that Jesus instructed his followers to avoid referring to themselves or others as teacher (Rabbi), lest the very social hierarchy he sought to overturn be reinstated by those who play at being in the know, as if only less-enlightened others need tutelage. There's something unseemly in speaking of learning in this way. Properly understood, there are no snobs on this road. Or as my friend Cory Robertson once put it, there is no hierarchy in poetry.

But the mysterious alchemy of learning—of awakening to ourselves—happens, and the least we can do is say so, letting people know, if we can, when they've helped us along, when they've somehow visualized, lyricized or said something that was in our heads. We get to testify concerning the how and the why of it, and I'm not sure we're quite alive to ourselves till we've begun to do so. With this in mind, every writing class I've taught—or presumed to try to teach—has begun with some variation of the question of how we might best go about *seeing* what we've seen. We are, each of us, libraries full of experience, sensations, words spoken for and against us, memories of joy and trauma, inexplicable scenes and unresolved stories. What insight might await us when we attempt to articulate it a little, when we begin to open up the book of what all's happened?

King Kong Burger

As I've noted, I find it uniquely unhelpful to divide the calls to worshipfulness I received in church settings from the ones I received via billboards, headphones and television screens. Marshall McLuhan tells us that when we distinguish entertainment from education we only demonstrate that we don't understand the first thing about either, and if religion names the stories that control us, awareness requires ample meditation on the instruction we've received and internalized. How is it, precisely, that we've been proselytized? Religion is in the details.

One early, formative memory of my own—as vivid as any Sunday school recollection—goes back to the time the Wendy's corporation (the Nashville franchise, anyway) once made life peculiarly difficult for my mother. At the age of six, I'd seen King Kong standing atop the World Trade Center with a flaming aircraft in one hand and a scantily clad Jessica Lange in the other, and somehow I knew he understood. It wouldn't be too long before I'd proudly sport the image on a metal lunchbox. But in those days of more primitive-feeling affiliations between the fast-food industry and the emerging phenomenon of blockbuster films, Wendy's had me at hello when they advertised their "King Kong Burger." The very name of the thing was enough to set me imagining any number of Kong-related products: a doll, a badge, a mask or even a figurine beneath the bun covered in ketchup and mustard. A true believer in Kong, I took them at their word. I needed to get to the nearest Wendy's without delay. My mother had seen the commercial and knew this trail of supposed associations to be a dead end, but my heart was set, so she facilitated the learning moment. She would show me what a "King Kong Burger" had to do with the King. We went, she paid up and we sat at a table together as I stared at the lumpen mess so utterly void of Kong. No semblance of Kong even on the wrapper. *In name only*, legally and literally, as advertised. The name, I was made to see, was a false witness. An unhappy meal. No satisfaction. Mostly a minimalist when it came to burgers, I couldn't even eat the thing. The con was on and it went way beyond Kong. She held my hand through the heartbreak.

The six-year-old would not have put it this way, but I'd received difficult instruction concerning the way advertised realities could so easily mess with my own longing for a world made richer by the likes of King Kong. And blessedly, given the love and the care that accompanied such well-orchestrated realizations, I was never made to feel ashamed of my reaching after that illusory something. Many Micronauts, Star Wars action figures and a slew of comic books would be demanded and provided in the years to come, but this particular epiphany would linger and take on the referential powers of a household anecdote. There are, after all, so many King Kong equivalents at every stage of human development as well as many a moment when the promise of a richer world hoped for comes true. I remember feeling I'd begun to offer something back in these exchanges the day I read *Watership Down* aloud to my mother on a long car trip. She was a captive audience, but I could tell she was really getting into it, visibly enjoying my enjoyment to the point that I felt it was hers, too. It was finally happening; I heard myself as a convincing teller of tales.

Catechism for the Day

Both of these episodes made it into my quiver of essentials because they're points along a trajectory without which I can't begin to explain myself to myself. I think too of the time a quiet and charmingly broody young woman in a high school art class saw fit to bestow upon me a mixtape of Suzanne Vega songs. Was it something I said? What had I done to indicate I was possibly a kindred spirit? The fact is I'm still trying to live up to this gesture, this vote of confidence that I might be, or prove to be, someone alive to what she sensed in Suzanne Vega. By crediting me in this way, it was as if she'd propelled me into a life more interesting.

"Tell me what you like and I'll tell you what you are," the Victorian-era art critic John Ruskin once decreed. This strikes me as both alarming and entirely true. What do I like and why? Really thinking that one through is as intensely telling as it would be to genuinely try to answer that profound question, "What are you into?" I'd have to begin with my attention collection, my book of common things, my working palette of lifelong recognitions. Looking at it honestly is a way of taking stock of the way my imagination's been formed and my behavior shaped, a chronicling of all that's somehow inspired confidence or a feeling of orienting knowingness within me. I'm also immediately reminded how unceasingly communal this process is. Literacy occurs between people, and it spreads one reading recommendation, one "You should check this out," one "I thought of you" and one playlist at a time. I'm the glad recipient, repeatedly, of myriad acts of intellectual hospitality on the part of people who've been kind enough to see within me an intelligence I have yet to access myself, people who saw fit to take me seriously by regarding me hopefully and imaginatively. Maybe you are too.

Given my frightened and lonely reading of the Bible—a common occurrence in the place that I come from—I was in serious need of such hospitality. I remember feeling weirdly elated by the fact of Robert De Niro reading 1 Corinthians 13 aloud in *The Mission*. It was as if one world was allowed to draw on another. Maybe it happened all the time. Maybe it was all one world. A damaging division, artificial as it was, was casually overcome by one more little pebble landing inside the wall I was in danger of building around myself, and I held on to it for dear life. I'd hear biblical references in INXS and A-ha lyrics. One source could speak to another as I spied a way to open my circle of affirmation a tiny bit to include more forms of human solidarity. I tend to believe this is how the good work gets done. I've been delivered from certain madness by certain loves. They're poetry and gospel—not that there's a tremendous difference between the two—to me.

And they're everywhere, these means whereby we begin to see what we're seeing. That which was unnamed gets suddenly put into words. That heavy happening never justly described or illuminated in our hearing finally receives fresh articulation and gets brought into the light of clear expression. A breakthrough occurs. It's what Shakespeare describes as imagination bodying forth the form of things heretofore unknown, conferring upon them tangible shapes and conjuring out of what used to be an airy, oft-debilitating nothing a local habitation and a name, a way of putting it.

To speak of one beloved format, this is the hope of the paleo-playlist, mixtape tradition, an early experience of mine in the giving, receiving and trading of attention collections. Here's a little something that orders my existence, we might say as we hand our enthusiasms over. It's a more time-consuming and tactile procedure than we're lately accustomed to in our age of social recommendation where a "like" or a tweet or an article posted online seems to sink to the bottom of the oceans of Internet within seconds, but it's the same communal impulse. Sharing what we're up to—what we believe we're discovering—with others is what stewards the possibility of friendship and revelation. It's the handing down and over—that's tradition—of what sacred intuition we hope we've accessed. How else do we access the meaning of our own experience? How else do we see what we've seen?

We're always being catechized in one way or another, and figuring out how the process has gone so far and might yet go is the lifetime work of religious awareness. To look hard at our attention collections—what's in there and why?—is to undertake the ancient imperative of the Delphic motto: Know thyself. Is this a task we still feel we can afford? Are people still up for doing this kind of thing? What kind of role do we want to have in our own daily catechesis?

I WAS RAISED CAPITALIST

In the song and dance I undertake as my teaching routine, I often suspect my primary duty is to alert students to the fact they've been catechized at all, that their religious formation is a living fact long underway as opposed to a phenomenon they can successfully get clear of and gaze upon with an air of detachment. And thus it befalls me to invite my students to begin to conceive religion, against popular wisdom, as a notion that might apply to their own lives as easily as it does to those who haven't made it this far in their supposed education. When they enter a university classroom, they have reason to believe that they're expected to leave the worrisome details of their particular religious backgrounds at the door lest they risk being perceived as narrow, backward or hopelessly biased. They're almost painfully well-catechized in the move most everyone in the westernizing world seems to want to make these days: *I'm not religious*. It's exceedingly difficult to discuss religion with people who are absolutely certain only other people have one.

How do we turn this ship around? "If religion is our subject, we'll have a much better time together," I observe, "and we'll have *a lot* more to talk about if we're willing to dare a little vulnerability and at least a smidgen of transparency concerning . . . would it help if we called it religious *baggage*? Are there ideas in and by which we were reared that we find it hard to—or even feel we mustn't—let go? I know there are. So please, let's not be stingy in sharing them.

Let's have a go at being openhanded. First written assignment? Describe *your* weird religious background.

"We all have one," I argue. "I'd be willing to bet many of you were probably raised capitalist, for instance." This somehow signals a clearing of the air and usually wins puzzled looks and a giggle or two. If we're going to deploy the idea of religion for all it's worth, we'll have to put everything on the table. We won't limit ourselves to talk about divinity or strange opinions concerning life after death; we're talking what's been normalized, learned behaviors and social formations, the shape of our enthusiasms, the ways we order our worlds, what we're hoping for in everything we're up to and the prickly question of what it is we genuinely decree essential—basically, the alarming realization of who we really are, that dramatic fact that rises to the surface in each of us for all to see, slowly and surely, a few days into the zombie apocalypse.

But the big reveal—*apocalypsis* is just Greek for revelation—of how it is we're in*formed*, what it is that constitutes our core concerns, need not await the appearance among us of the walking dead. We can begin to think about that one now, and perhaps we should. That would be the amazing aphorism—perhaps worthy of a tattoo—dropped upon us by Albert Camus by way of his narrator, Jean-Baptiste Clamence, in his novel *The Fall*: "I'll tell you a big secret, *mon cher*. Don't wait for the Last Judgment. It takes place every day."[1]

Game on. Why not take a look at what we're into, those patterns of behavior we're often immersed in so thoroughly and hypnotically that we have to fight for the right to even think about them? Let's look hard together. We're welcome to say whatever we want to about all the things we believe, but any sacred tradition we care to reference will remind us that the surest evidence of what we believe is what we do. Faith without works is . . . not actually your faith, as it turns out. We do what we believe—maybe it's a relief to even say it aloud—and we *don't* do what we don't. It's no secret after all.

If what you believe is what you say and do, the guiding provocation runs like this: Show me your receipts, your text messages,

> **The surest evidence of what we believe is what we do.**

your gas mileage, your online history, a record of your daily doings and, just to get things started, a transcript of the words you've spoken aloud in the course of a single day, and *then* we might begin to get a picture of your religious commitments. What doors of perception might begin to open when we allow ourselves to look at religion—and our own lives—in this way? What personal hypocrisies do we keep obscured to ourselves when we don't?

The space of your worship is the space of your life. It's all made plain in the details of every kind of personal investment. A worship *service*? We're welcome to schedule them as often as we like, but it won't mean our worship stops or starts according to our schedules. The living witness of what we do with our lives speaks even as it writes out our detailed histories, and it doesn't operate according to all those ultimately unsustainable compartmentalizations we use to fool ourselves and others. No blind trusts, we might say, in the playing out of my religion.

LABOR WELL THE MINUTE PARTICULARS

But we begin with attention collections. There's no religious tradition apart from some form of canonization after all. So why not begin considering religion by way of our own personal canons? Every class is an opportunity to, in some sense, simultaneously present my attention collection to students each day—in truth, I already wanted to do that anyway—and to urge them to become more alertly appreciative and aware of their own. We all have them—I manage to keep myself from shouting—these lines, memories, advertisements, shows, songs and scenarios we go to instinctively, because we find them convincing, meaningful, comforting and maybe somehow weirdly clarifying. And there's a reason—so many reasons—they're there. Let's explore them. Let's have a go at sharing the intelligence we've gathered. As long as we're here, let's somehow expand the space of the talkaboutable together.

Inevitably, I detect resistance, so I begin to show my hand. Everyone knows songs, so we go around the room naming our favorite—or *a* favorite—musical artist. Even then, there's a tangible unwillingness to risk getting caught feeling too fervently in favor of . . . Someone? Anything? It's as if it's a source of shame or something. I'm last and I usually go for broke. I like Radiohead. Or to put it more specifically, I *believe* Radiohead. In truth, I'm persuaded by them. Their take on the world enriches my own, making me more alive to myself and others, more attentive to what William Blake calls the minute particulars, the oft-overlooked, on-the-ground details that make up the lives we lead. Anyone who hopes to do good to another person, according to Blake, will have to attend to—"labour well"—the minute particulars, minutely particularizing their so-called love. Radiohead is an ever-present help in the trouble I meet when I try my hand at the work of loving well by loving specifically. They call upon me—perhaps you can hear the call too—to immerse *my soul* in love. Radiohead. I drink their Kool-Aid.

As it turns out, not every college student feels the love for Radiohead, but testifying unrestrainedly serves to prepare a table of expectation in the wilderness. We're going to attempt to be present to one another by owning aloud our own interests and enthusiasms, reflecting on the art which, in Kafka's phrase, is (or was) the ice ax striking at the frozen sea inside us. What voices somehow get through and why? It's often a tall order for most, but it's also an invitation to become more deeply aware of what's going on in our minds, to take ourselves more seriously and, most important, to feel our own worth. Holding out an artifact or two from our attention collections is a very good place to start. By doing so, we take the measure of our own education.

A river of hypocrisy and denial probably runs through it, I'm sure, but my attention collection bends toward social righteousness, the celebration of right relations, the lively critique—sometimes a comedic skewering—of wrong relations and the reaching out for better ones. It covers a lot of territory: Aretha Franklin singing "R-E-S-P-E-C-T," *The Simpsons*, Alan Moore's *Watchmen*, Emily Dickinson, *Twin Peaks*, Wendell Berry, John Hughes films, Laurie Anderson, all manner of human goodness. I take these witnesses to heart and, in no small way, measure my life by them. I'd be squandering the gift of consciousness they give me were I to keep it all to myself, hiding it under a bushel, as it were, getting lost in my hopeless little screen. What good is a revelation if we refuse to publicize it? Who wants to laugh or shake a fist at injustice or experience an insight all by themselves?

I collect and share what I feel I've been given in the way of illumination. I find myself compiling, tweaking, amending and constantly reconfiguring. It's a process we're all up to in one way or another. It's a mental journal I need desperately to help me to wake up from the hypnosis I know to be possible and even likely in the sometimes weary world too often prone to tantrums. And in this sense, my attention collection might be my primary way of being social, of having something hopeful to give people when I happen upon them, something that might somehow overcome whatever initially appears to divide us from one another.

BRING FORTH WHAT IS WITHIN YOU

I presume this is the kind of task Jack Kerouac had in mind when he expressed his desire to be a great rememberer, someone who manages, from time to time, to redeem life from darkness by re-membering well, by *re*membering people, places and experiences truly, wholly and holily. Broad is the path of *dis*membering, and narrow is the gate of righteous remembering. But there remains the duty to chronicle the life and liveliness we witness in the hope of preserving and passing on visions that sustain despite the reigning distortions, visions that hold everything dear. We know the fear-driven pressure to reduce, to control and to cut everything and everyone down to manageable size. This too is religion, and its calls to worship are everywhere. But true religion, remembering well amid the haste, hurry and distraction of the average day, requires a conscious effort. Being an ecstatic affirmer, a noticer supreme, is a full-time job.

Such remembering is anything but a turning away from the world; it's the servicing and handing on of visions that lend our lives coherence against that which degrades and destroys. What Kerouac means to heed himself and issue to all within earshot is the call to creative literacy, that conscientious communality of which we're all capable, the call to steward our own experience, to not be indifferently absorbed in our own lives, the sweet burden of thinking socially.

Kerouac wasn't the first to have a go at being a poet-prophet. There's a long history of folks trying to be one more person upon whom very little is lost. Most are anonymous, but they hold the world carefully in their generous hands. We might say all are called, in some way, to keep the faith by way of intense attentiveness. As accounts of the Beat Generation's history have it, Allen Ginsberg once handed an early attempt at a poem to Kerouac, who read it delightedly, observing, "See? You can do it too."

This is the form that *taking care* takes. And we can't really do it with our arms folded tight. It's the generosity upon which the human species depends, and as an unendingly communal activity, it always and ever requires a village. As the food critic voiced by Peter O'Toole (aptly named Anton Ego) in *Ratatouille* wisely and humbly observes in wide-awake awareness of his own inescapably social vocation, "The new needs friends."

If we're beginning to accept the work of always cultivating our attention collections with care as a kind of cultural obligation, I'd like to push the notion even further by observing that it might be more helpfully held as a sacred necessity. If I'm not in the habit of consciously exercising my own imagination, there are armies of con artists with many a King Kong equivalent who are more than willing to do it for me, to capitalize on my neuroses at every turn.

What is more, the barricaded mind is a dangerous one. A saying attributed to Jesus in the Gospel of Thomas puts the matter starkly: "If you bring forth what is within you, what you bring forth will save you. If you do not bring forth what is within you, what you do not bring forth will destroy you." Or as Steve Earle once put it to that endlessly beleaguered soul named Bubbles on *The Wire*: "You gotta let it out to let it go."

THE MIRACLE OF ATTENTIVENESS

In this sense, the act of self-expression, putting our stories, our jams, our beloved enthusiasms on the table, isn't just an essential practice of self-preservation, it also creates the possibility of neighborliness, a meaning-making exercise in the work of being a human being among human beings. In my own stumbling efforts to draw my children into a wakefulness of hearing, sharing and carefully following the stories that surround us, I was recently schooled by my son, Sam, who'd skipped straight to an insight I had yet to reach: "So literacy is about cooperating with people?"

Undoubtedly. I would also say it's the most joyous game in town. In the long haul, literacy is a lifelong practice of attentiveness, of really believing in the strange actuality of other humans whose lives might speak persuasively and blessedly into your own. As Guy Davenport reminds us, our attention collections are the stomping grounds of art: "Art happens in an act of attention . . . that is to be transferred, after being made into an intelligible shape, to other minds. We forget that this is a miracle."

This is the joy of experiencing our own lives and those of others without defensiveness, to see and say what we're haunted by, what we cherish and why. True religion requires it. It's a group work, of course. If we deny or repress our attention collections, hiding them away from the bright light of day, we diminish ourselves and likely anyone who might dare to try to be in relationship with us in our guarded states.

But if we value what we're up to and into enough to celebrate and share it, we're no longer closed off to the genius of others, and our isolation is overcome by the heartening presence of community. The more we share what we're into with candor and openness while inviting and allowing other people to return the favor, really receiving the input we've perhaps been secretly hoping for all along, the richer and more varied our attention collections become.

Which is why I think it right to hold our collections out to one another with open hands. We get to share and reflect upon our source materials together. I wouldn't have much of one to begin with without the gifts, the urgings, the recommendations, the unconscious instruction of so many. "I think you might like this" is my love language. It's an indication that someone's noticed me and given enough thought to the shape of my affections to imagine they've found something they suspect might speak to me. It also means they've gone ahead and loved something enough to get a little evangelistic about it. I'm always looking for a word of inspiration, a better take on reality.

Who doesn't want *that*? Who *isn't* running down a dream and hoping it might lead to a better vision for inhabiting the world hopefully? Well, it's complicated. We have ever before us so many false witnesses to sift out from the true, so many schemes that prey on the reigning disorientation many of us feel most of the time, so

many false signals mixed in among the true and therefore revelatory witnesses. Nevertheless, the miracle of attentiveness is
passed down and handed over and bandied about one poem, one
podcast, one Bible study, one book club at a time. It's what there is.

But we have to show up for these things. We have to contemplate
the film or the album before forming a judgment upon it. We have
to read to the bottom of the article. We have to see the witness, get
the drift, before we can begin to reject or receive it. Discerning,
processing and passing on the gift of attentiveness takes time. If a
tradition is a never-ending hand-me-down, we have to sit still and
even meditate a little to figure out what enriches, what needs to be
rejected or what we'll do well to rethink a little. In the case of any
story or song, it will take time to see clearly and actually witness
what a tradition was trying to hand down in its context *then* before
we can begin to experience what it might hand down *now*. Real affection will involve investment and follow-up. It might not even
feel like work. I believe it's best understood and undertaken as
a form of joy.

> **Conscious cultivation of
> our own thought life is
> a sacred necessity.**

And again, conscious cultivation of our own thought life
is a sacred necessity, nothing less than a determined involvement
in our own controlling story, our own religious formation. Why not
be conscious participants in our own catechesis? The catechesis,
we understand, is happening whether we choose to engage it or not
and, as ever, we're alarmingly free to look hard, at any time, at what
we've learned, what we're learning and what we might do well to
unlearn. What's been normalized—woefully or beautifully—and
why? Are there untapped resources for being transformed by the
ongoing renewal of our minds instead of being led around by fear
and anxiety and the everyday denials that accompany them? What
choices might deeper consciousness require?

3

Choose your ancestors carefully

It's hard to overstate how deep the need can get for things to make sense.

Sean Phillips in John Darnielle's
Wolf in White Van

A REMARKABLE AND DISTURBING *Saturday Night Live* skit from the twentieth century often comes to mind as a treasured touchstone in my attention collection. It features Will Ferrell most prominently as he harnesses that sense of raw human madness he snaps into like nobody else. As I measure these things, it achieves a degree of comedic perfection, prophetic in its way, as it lampoons and even revels in the fracturing of an alleged orderliness upon which social relations seem to depend. What happens when the given script of what's appropriate is suddenly unavailable? What will we do with ourselves?

It's the carefully scripted celebration of the twentieth-anniversary episode of a Phoenix-based morning show called *Wake Up and Smile*.[1] As the opening theme song fades, Ferrell and his co-anchor, played by Nancy Walls, get the show underway and exchange pleasantries with David Alan Grier as the friendly weatherman. They laugh and smile and agree that their decades-long work together "has *definitely* been a fun ride." But the transition into the cooking tips portion of the show is suddenly interrupted by the failure of essential technology, or, as Ferrell's man-in-charge puts it: "The teleprompter . . . on which everything we say appears on . . . is broken. . . . We're having what is known in the business as . . . technical times." Amid a dawning sense of panic and heavy breathing, Ferrell and Walls are urged by those behind the camera to undertake the impossibly unexpected labor of ad-libbing.

"You know . . ." Ferrell begins with a blank, anxious stare into his own inner resources. "I had a notion the other day."

"Well," she responds approvingly. "Um . . . Notions make this country . . . happen."

What notion arises from Ferrell's raw feed? "I . . . I was thinking someone should get a group together . . . with guns to sweep out those ghettos." And before he can take the words back, we cut to a commercial break.

Upon returning, the hosts are holding their positions, looking around helplessly, clutching their armrests and spouting off inanities arising from deep within their hearts. Walls: "I . . . drive a red car." Ferrell: "Make sure those poor people stay away from it. They've got swords." Grier: "Fear. I must control the fear. Please. *Someone tell me what to say.*"

Nervously taking up the mantle of "the dominant one," Ferrell flails in the direction of what he believes their situation must require: "Easy. . . . Easy. If we panic, we die! . . . We must use the furniture to build a barricade." Taking apart the set to defend against every imagined threat, his coanchor's barely articulate complaints of feeling cold, hungry and alone ("There's no words!"), and the weatherman's desperate pleas to an unknown "They" who, if they all wait patiently, might see fit to *give back the words*, Ferrell lets out an agonized scream abruptly cut off by another commercial.

It's all downhill from here, and it goes—alarmingly—over the top. Their minutes of lawlessness yield torches, a beheading, a turtle on loan from the zoo they're now determined to consume for nourishment, and a shirtless Will Ferrell with a black handprint on his chest loudly decreeing, "The order of the hand will rule!" And just as gore and chaos have conquered all hope of restoration, the teleprompter is online again, *the words have returned* and our presenters are expected to snap back to their trusty old composed routine. Through blood, sweat and tears of anguish and gratitude, our hosts try to deflect attention from the horror they've wrought while unscripted as they try to find their way back to their previously in progress celebration, under dictation, of "twenty magical years of *Wake Up and Smile.*"

I'm not entirely sure why this ridiculous skit delights me so. What is it that so thrills me in the exaggerated, hypercaricatured portrayal of the breakdown of the social contract? Why do I see so much beauty in the breakdown? Do I really imagine this particular live footage of late-night song and dance is, in some deep sense, somehow telling the truth?

I'll readily admit that I do. When I find myself sitting quietly and nodding knowingly among a group of people being addressed—or trying to appear as if they're being addressed—by someone else, I often hear the words of the great and powerful Oz arising ineluctably in my mind: "Pay no attention to the man behind the curtain." I worry over what forms of conscience, soul and liveliness might get suppressed or somehow evaded when things are expected to take a turn for the formal. I wonder what spirit is made to flee—and what different spirit is made to enter in—when we clear our throats to signal that *now . . .* we're getting down to business. What transition do we *think* we're staging? What did we leave behind, and where are we supposedly going in the guise of our somehow suddenly serious—as if by magic—selves? Who are we kidding?

THE SOCIAL PIPELINE

This twenty-year-old skit poses the crucial question of where we really are apart from the social cues, prompts and stage directions by which we figure out how to assure one another we can be trusted, reasoned with and counted on to not behave like sociopaths. It makes comically plain our desperate desire to know what it is we're supposed to be doing, but what if that's *all* we're doing? What if, like Tolstoy's Ivan Ilyich, our lifelong commitment to discerning and performing what's *considered* to be socially acceptable is precisely where we're stalled in our development, never seriously asking the essential question of whether what's *expected* of us in our day-to-day existence is what's right? What if that which is celebrated, championed and praised in our particular milieu is, as it turns out, an all-pervading social darkness we've come to accept and look to as light? Perhaps we're interested in finding out. Maybe we've met some people who appear to be interested in such questions. Maybe we could make a community out of it. Maybe it's already there, waiting for us.

Very weirdly, we have it on ancient authority that the intellectual burden of pursuing these questions is a much less onerous task than the psychic burden we take on ourselves the more we try to avoid the questions. We have Socrates, of course, who tells us that the unexamined life is hardly worth the effort, but it's Jesus of Nazareth I'm thinking of. He insists that his instruction, in spite of all the ways it overturns the social conventions of his day and our own, is actually an easier yoke and a lighter burden than what we're accustomed to taking on in our feverish avoidance of what real neighborliness, in word and deed, might require. There is so much to overcome in the work of seeing rightly, but a good joke, when we receive it *feelingly*, can jump our defenses in an instant. Consider Will Ferrell's poor, exhausted anchor looking hard at the static deep within and finding nothing save poor people coming at him with swords. The sham is tiring. Peer pressure is forever. Figuring out what you have to do and say and believe—or pretend to believe—to get by can wear a body out. Playing along with the farce will leave you fatigued.

"Come out from among it!" one can almost hear a comedy, an accurate song, a good teacher or a thing of beauty say. Step away from the sham. Act natural. Act natural? If only it were so simple. We find it's an everyday do-over distinguishing light from darkness, because at the heart of any sham is a desire to be social, an easily deformed one but a desire nonetheless, a desire to be *a part of* something instead of feeling alone and *apart from* everything and everyone. It can go very badly, even taking a turn for the murderous, but it's a sacred longing and it must not be despised. A moment's consideration will afford us any number of examples of the ways our heart's desire to be social—to count, to be heard, to somehow matter—is enlisted, exploited, preyed upon and harnessed repeatedly to maximize financial profits. But honoring it with honesty, mercy, candor and kindness might be the soul of seriousness itself.

"I wanna go someplace where we know somebody who can plug us into the social pipeline." As far as I can tell, there's isn't a woman or man alive who isn't somehow

> **Step away from the sham.**

spoken for in these words from *Dumb and Dumber*, offered with desperate longing to Harry Dunne (Jeff Daniels) by Lloyd Christmas (Jim Carrey), a man for whom a murdered parakeet has come to serve as a final straw, a sacred sign indicating that it's high time the two men finally set out to make something of themselves. Even if we somehow wave it away out of disgust or despair to get a little distance from it, "the social pipeline" remains maddeningly in view for everyone, still staring us down in one way or another. Not a bad name for the state of play, but how will this work? Are dignity and self-possession still a thing? How do we avoid entering yet again or, as we often find ourselves doing, unwittingly perpetuating one more sham? Is the pursuit of true religion—right thought and right action—even possible?

I like to think of thinking—*really* thinking—as a party to which everyone is invited. It's a party where we have much to talk about and share, but it also involves being alive to the dangers of not really listening, to the living death *not* listening is, as we know we have to hold our favorite ideas about ourselves and others lightly. We often have to let to go to really see, to give way, to allow for the unexpected wisdom of others, to see that we're not seeing. There's a way of envisioning people, a way of talking about ourselves, that invites us to really *take care*, an intensely attentive hospitality so wary of the dangers of distorted thinking that it won't allow the social pipeline, for instance, to be perceived or portrayed as some kind of zero-sum game.

HUMAN LEARNING IS NOT OWNED

Way back in the twentieth century, I witnessed an exchange that stayed with me as a kind of standard for what I'm talking about. I was in my third year of teaching high school English, staring blankly at a copier in the "Teacher's Work Room," when a student walked in to retrieve something or other for someone in authority.

"Hey!" a colleague shouted in a mock-bully tone. "What are you doing in here? How *dare* you impersonate a teacher!"

The student rolled her eyes and moved along, but a nearby faculty member seized the moment to say something subversively helpful: "Isn't that what we're all doing?"

What a saving rhetorical question, this casual assertion that all the world is, after all, something of a stage with each of us sometimes poorly, sometime persuasively, putting on our sincere acts of make-believe and hoping for the best. I suppose I'm always a little heartened by a bemused word of self-deprecation from someone in the thick of things, a wink that acknowledges the sense in which we're all shamming our way through life. But the moment probably lingered longer because of the wide-eyed response I received when I recounted the exchange to a friend who taught at another high school: "No one would *ever* say that at my school."

What an unfortunate environment to imagine. No adult allowed to wonder aloud if you're a pretender? No honest expression of confusion permitted? No voicing the very-worth-asking question of whether education is genuinely occurring in the hours we share with students? No openness to the possibility that perhaps every so often, the service we were supposedly rendering wasn't even remotely carrying over, that we weren't *actually* teaching?

So much can get lost in the theatrics of expertise, of trying to make an impression, of trying to demand—as if it were possible—respect. And that quieter work of living out a vocation—knowing and enjoying what we're good at and experiencing the thrill of doing it well—can get buried in that all-too-religious commitment to keep up appearances. The subtler question of presence, of how to go about being meaningfully present to people and how to be alive to the living presence of others, will often go unasked.

My memory of that incident returned to me recently when I overheard an English professor friend, Annette Sisson, casually posit a revolutionary saying that begins to thaw something within me whenever I recall it: "Human learning is not owned." Ah yes, how could I have forgotten such a fact when I feel it in my bones? What a helpful way of conceiving of education. Learning is a communal movement, and it won't easily abide a restlessly egotistical acquisitiveness or a nervous clawing after competitive advantage. Of course, in the ongoing effort to be a good steward of my own realizations, I might do well to try to own or *own up to* them, but it's never as if I have only my own isolated self to thank for whatever I manage to realize. Like any form of meaning, learning largely happens by way of the mental labor of others whether dead or alive, passed down, gingerly handed over and sometimes *possibly* facilitated—I'd like to think—by one person sharing his or her attention collection with another. People come to consciousness in relationship. This is the phenomenon—oh, how it enlivens a heart!—of shared meaning. It takes two to mean, after all. And no one has meaning alone.

Religion Is Not a Fixed Script

All learning is shared learning. All insight is *communally* transmitted. All eloquence is borrowed. There is no wisdom you've gleaned for which you don't have some someone else to thank. Your understanding of your own world has come to you—and will keep coming to you—by the hands of others. It's been *traditioned* unto you. If we'd like to, we're welcome to describe an awareness of this state of affairs as a *religious* awareness, but I'm not sure what the application of the adjective adds to plain old awareness. Religion, like stories, promises and rituals, is just one more social fact. It happens to us. The *what* of what happened is the actual content of *what* got traditioned, the marching orders you've found yourself following. It's what's been ingrained in your thinking. Do you like what's been ingrained in your thinking? Would you like to see it turned around, transformed or revolutionized? Do you feel stuck?

It's a beautiful and wondrous thing to recall that a person's religion need not be a fixed script. While it may be the case that, beginning within the womb, we learn by way of pattern recognitions, mimicking what's being modeled for us, looking to have our patterns and models confirmed and reconfirmed, we're also often made to discover that many paradigms to which we're prone to clutch are, in fact, faulty, and our thinking undergoes a sacred shift. Salvation comes to our household. It's not even an especially rare happening. As wandering pilgrims always in search of a more coherent story, we can change, convert, reform and stumble into new habits of being at any given moment. People can wake up to themselves at any time. We aren't, as it turns out, irredeemably stuck. Or as the novelist Ralph Ellison once remarked, we may very well be *stuck* with our relatives, but we get to *choose* our ancestors.[2] There's no denying the fact of our particular lineage, however embarrassing and dysfunctional it might be, but we can step into or draw from a different, more life-giving trajectory whenever we please.

What Ellison is referring to specifically is his refusal, especially as a young black artist, to allow anyone to constrain his range of influences, the hodgepodge that would make up his inner creative core, his source material, his attention collection. According to popular dictates, he was expected to have certain influences like Langston Hughes and Richard Wright, but he insisted on adopting and holding close to his heart particular ancestors like Faulkner, Hemingway and T. S. Eliot in constant defiance of what had been placed before him as appropriate categories and genres. He felt himself free to draw inspiration from anyone he liked: "I learned very early that in the realm of the imagination all people and their ambitions and their interests could meet."[3] In this sense, we're perfectly free to write our own ticket at any time, to choose our own traditions as we discern which voices, tales and creative offerings might serve us well in becoming what we long to be, to receive the witness of others, whether near or far, by making *their* witness a part of our own. As individuals, we each have an alarmingly profound degree of personal power in preparing within ourselves certain inner resources from which we can constantly draw, certain dreams in our hearts that won't leave us alone. We'll want to choose our ancestors carefully, because we don't have to wait for the teleprompter to break to discover what's in there, what reserves we have or don't have in the work of keeping it together, imagining our neighbors righteously and, generally speaking, playing well with others. We can follow up or track down any question or insight we'd like at any time with honesty and energy, and we're right to do so because our inner life is always underway. And so much will depend on the channels to which we choose to remain tuned in.

You never hear people put it this way, and I don't intend to start a trend, but when we consider the ever-evolving process of a person's thinking, the way a person imagines and organizes the world, it could almost seem appropriate to ask each other from time to time, How's your religion coming along? How's *it* going? Born again, or the same old, same old? Did you successfully distinguish darkness from light in the course of your day? Is there a fever in your mind that won't go away? Mind if I prescribe a poem?

If certain organizing fictions or controlling stories are inevitable vehicles of human culture (and culture—like religion—is an insanely large abstraction big enough to include the big ideas behind the big behavior, the big buildings and the big blowups that we're trying to somehow account for with words), a self-conscious grappling over what actually animates us might be the most essential, sacred task any of us can take on. No human development—what a phrase—without it. What am I up to and why? Who are my ancestors, and why am I choosing them?

We Are What We Pretend to Be

Another way of putting these questions—and if it helps, we can feel free to call it THE QUESTION OF OUR LIVES—is this: What are the movements, *the ancestral lines*, within and along which we'd like, or hope, to find our own lives in deep continuity? It might be important to add, for emphasis, *because they already are*. It's already the case that our values—the ones we have, and probably not the ones we expend vast amounts of energy trying to appear to have—are visible via the value judgments we make all day every day. It might involve a little digging, but a thumbnail sketch is already possible. You'll know us by our fruit, as that peasant artisan prophet again reminds us. Certain themes are, no doubt, already apparent. Like it or not, the claim, the call, the continuities along which my own lived existence sits can probably be reasonably guessed at even now. I myself often hope, for instance, that someone might be able to say of me that my seeking of God's reign and righteousness wasn't entirely theoretical, that my story somehow also told, from time to time, the old, old story of Jesus and his love.

Of course, this road is fraught with many a paradox. Pick an ancient or contemporary source of wisdom, and you'll be told to avoid self-consciousness, to not let the right hand know what the left hand is doing, to lose your life in order to find it and to do good in secret lest you find yourself doing it *to be seen* doing it. "We are what we pretend to be," instructs Vonnegut, "so we must be careful about what we pretend to be."[4] Can this provocatively Oscar-Wildean adage be taken up helpfully?

I certainly think so. I believe we take it up whenever we follow up on our own loves well, *knowingly* drawing inspiration from people and ideas we find beautiful and imitating them like wide-eyed children do. If comparison is the thief of joy, then perhaps curiosity *without* undue comparison *plus* wonder can equal inspiration.[5] We know inspiration when we're exposed to what feels like a saving bit of information, when we see, hear or experience another person and find ourselves longing to know what they seem to know so wisely and well. This too is the social pipeline. How do we level with ourselves with good humor and humility concerning our own longing for meaning? We can begin by letting ourselves wonder why it is that *this* and not *that* seems to resonate. A commitment to becoming aware of what's going on in your mind requires confession, certainly, but it's also a matter of taking careful stock of what's within your bag of treasured things, your attention collection. There's no getting away from the equation that is the ineluctable relation between your output and your input.

I think too of the Catholic anarchist activist Dorothy Day, whose commitment to the love of God took the form of holding all things in common with the disenfranchised poor in houses of hospitality still at large in the Catholic Worker movement. She often passed time in prison, whether for protesting American war making or demanding a woman's right to vote. She refused the rush on the part of onlookers to decree her a saint because she sensed that, behind the compliment, there lurked the suggestion that only some people are called to the alleged extremes of Christian practice: "Don't call me a saint; I don't want to be dismissed so easily." How would she like to be remembered then? As someone who read the novels of Dostoevsky well.

This formulation of aspiration gets at the question of ancestral lines extremely well. We get to reach out to those voices that have reached out to us, and by doing so we extend their reach even further. One could observe, for instance, that Dostoevsky's life was, from at least a few angles, an unmitigated disaster of addiction, betrayal and no small amount of anti-Semitism. But if Day's witness to his witness is to be believed, his own creative faithfulness to his novelistic visions of a broken world can't be separated from one of the most persuasive prophetic movements of our time. His feats of attentiveness attended to hers in the very way that, if we want them to, hers will attend to ours. In the realm of the prophetic imagination, everybody's profoundest, most lyrical longings for the world can be made to meet up with everybody else's. There remain so many ways to say—to testify concerning—who and what rings true.

TASTE AND SEE

Once you begin to see it this way, these shout-outs are visible everywhere. It's the ongoing paying of tribute, the acknowledgment of sources, that leads to many an homage that can't help but articulate yet another mental breakthrough, another instance in which one person's creative effort somehow releases the creative capacities of another's. In R.E.M.'s "E-Bow the Letter," Michael Stipe extends the high-five of gratitude to Patti Smith, for whom it's often as if her every song, story or poem is a clear-eyed, ecstatic expression of thanksgiving to someone else. Bob Dylan's "Last Thoughts on Woody Guthrie" doesn't name Guthrie until the very end of a very long poem, but, by the end, the sanity-saving service Guthrie rendered to Dylan is abundantly evident. Human beings everywhere and in every time make it past or through or to the end of their long loneliness by believing other human beings who pass their own inspirations down through a long chronicling of plainspeak, of trying to say what they see. One true believer after another. Or as Dylan once put it on the subject of his life's work, "I believe the songs."[6]

Needless to say, I don't think of this as an evasion of creed, community or doctrine. I would hope that we are all collectors and believers of good stories, songs and all manner of artfulness. It is in so many ways the good work to be done. We get to stand by our jams with our very lives, living up to them somehow as gifts of discernment. We don't receive them at all till we do. How else would a body go about tasting and seeing that life or even the Lord of life is good? We can stare at reality for a lifetime without seeing it, but we learn to see it better, more righteously, when we choose our ancestors well, when we pick up and examine what they placed in the path for our everlasting benefit.

And they—our ancestors—really did collect and set all kinds of things down to pass along for our approval, saving them and treasuring them, one feat of attentiveness at a time, for the joy of someone else treasuring what they found sacred. The hope of civilization resides in the attention collections of the many unknowns to whose powers of canonization we owe so much. So much goodness has been carried over. We get to pass it on too. The poet Mary Rose O'Reilly describes the process aptly: "People all over the world are doing very hard things—turning the other cheek, giving all they have to the poor, eating potatoes without salt—because some confused and yawning student took a note."[7] We live off the generosity of those who pay heed. Will we answer the call to do so ourselves?

THE WAY OF THE GIFT

There is so much that distracts us from doing so and from even having a sense of how to begin, but the urge to make meaning persists. One of the chief obstacles to treasuring the insights available to us in the relentlessly communal work of waking up to ourselves and others is also a primary target of this book: the defensive mechanism of disassociation when it comes to what we think we have in hand when we say "religion." Rightly understood, it's a cue for renewed curiosity concerning what we're doing with ourselves, for what others seem to be about at their core and a cause for wonder. Why cling to an alleged *non* religiousness as if it were a life-preserver against the complications of other people? Is there a lasting refuge in disassociation?

Believing there might be is understandable given the mess of things we've inherited under the moniker of religion. Understandable to a point, I should say. And I'm helped here by the wisdom of the character John Ames, a seventy-six-year-old Iowan pastor in Marilynne Robinson's novel *Gilead*, which is a long diary written by Ames to a son whose young adulthood he knows he won't live to see. He worries that his son might fall into the disassociating rush, as many have done and will do when it comes to church community, excommunicating themselves on account of the church's dysfunction but also on the presumption that the dysfunction outside it is somehow lesser and the counsel on offer elsewhere somehow wiser. Ames, as the latest and likely last of a long line of pastors, offers no defense of the church's failings, but he seizes the occasion to express a broader vision for the way he hopes his son might come to understand the church's witness and the disillusionment that often accompanies it.

He begins by noting that as a child he himself was possessed by a naive but telling misimpression of the metal steeples of churches. He presumed that churches everywhere nobly affixed crosses at great heights to absorb the lightning that might otherwise endanger smaller structures in their communities, purposefully seeking to take the hit in a gesture of communal gallantry. He came to know better and to understand that not all churches were situated on the Great Plains, that not all pastors were like his father and that many a supposed church community falls woefully short of what could be rightly called Christian practice. He wants his son to understand that he's exceedingly aware of this fact. He knows that there is so much anyone with a conscience must decry in that which passes for church and that his own experience of the church has been limited and unique "in many senses" and perhaps "in every sense." But in this he allows himself and his reader to be a crucially important everybody-everywhere, *unless*:

> Unless it really is a universal and transcendent life, unless the bread is the bread and the cup is the cup everywhere, in all circumstances, and it is a time with the Lord in Gethsemane that comes for everyone, as I deeply believe. . . . It all means more than I can tell you. So you must not judge what I know by what I find words for. If I could only give you what my father gave me. No, what the Lord has given me and must also give you. But I hope you will put yourself in the way of the gift.[8]

Say what you must about your inheritance. Perhaps you'll feel called upon to betray it in more ways than one. But put yourself—*keep* yourself—in the way of the gift at all cost. Understand the joy and the obligation to carry what goodness there is in it forward. This admonition is at the heart of the sensibility I hope to urge upon others in regard to our talk of religion. It's a disposition that allows for disaffection but also disallows the prejudgment that amounts to preemptive excommunication of others, those ignorant souls concerning whose beliefs we're all too prone to believe have somehow already reached the shallow bottom. Ames hopes his son will know to place himself in the way—the path—of the gift in all things, including the possibility that his own father was a steward of a sacred mystery for which words will often—must even necessarily—fail. Because it's in the nature of a gift, the offering and the reception, to create relationship and to overcome that which divides, one can't remain in the way of the gift and also definitively disassociate. When a gift occurs, we see ourselves in others, our very lives sustained by the grace of others, and we find we can hardly hold ourselves apart. The gift occasions communion, that wholeness for which we're all longing in one way or another most of the time.

What are we to do with our craving for order and meaning? Stay in the way of the gift. Consider all that might yet come to you—all that might yet remain in circulation *by way of* you—as a living tradition. Stay within the line of its movement. Make something of it. Make it available. We know well the burden of being a member (letting yourself be *re*membered) within a community, but there are also times we might, at any moment, begin—or begin again—to experience this burden as a gift.

> **What are we to do with our craving for order and meaning? Stay in the way of the gift.**

And this again places us firmly within a particular paradox, because without the burden of belonging in some way to other people, we have no way of experiencing ourselves *as* a gift to others. At such times, our deep desire to be telling and following a story, to be of help and to share our enthusiasms with somebody—anybody—is without anything we can see as a genuine outlet. Without the flow of the gift, we have no access to the social pipeline, no means of making sense of ourselves. What are we to do with the mad turbulence of our own self-consciousness? Consider the gift.

INTERNATIONAL WATERS WITH IMAGINARY LINES ON THEIR SURFACE

"It's hard to overstate how deep the need can get for things to make sense," observes the reclusive forty-something narrator, Sean Phillips, in John Darnielle's *Wolf in White Van*.[9] And in my thinking and hoping concerning the way of the gift, he often arises in my mind as a kind of test case, a frontier of longing, sadness and good humor. A recent addition to my attention collection, I think of him as a dark marvel and a gift to my understanding of myself and to others of my generation.

The story of the gunshot wound that left his face grotesquely disfigured at seventeen is only completely spelled out on the final page of the novel, but even as we're deprived till then of certain details, we're made to see that his will to matter and his will to mean can't be isolated from this event. As a teenager with a love for *Conan the Barbarian* paperbacks, late-night televangelist programs, Dungeons and Dragons and the coin-operated video game Xevious ("Playing it was like watching flowers bloom"[10]), his chosen ancestors are, at first blush, unconventional and, by popular estimate, unworthy. But Phillips bestows upon each such depth and lyricism that his passionate pilgrimage leaves his parents and most of his peers in a pale of lukewarm denial. He is alive—eye-rubbingly alive—to the minute particulars around him and the beauty, the goodwill and the subtle but devastating hypocrisies he's expected to take on as his own in what passes for the real world. As early as sixth grade and into his earning of a modest income officiating a mail-order role-playing game called Trace Italian, Phillips is a purveyor and seeker of "true vision,"[11] and his tragic situation renders him an extraordinarily keen observer of the human drama even as it mostly excludes him. It's as if he takes people individually and every pop-culture artifact placed before him more seriously than they take themselves. Though pulled into despair by the delusions and denials normalized within his family, he pushes through with a tender and affectionate determination to see them rightly: "I try to be careful about the things I think."[12] It takes courage to see sometimes.

He finds his attention held by the memory of a child's voice on the beach in a commercial for a game called Stay Alive ("I'm the sole survivor!") and the way certain words seem to address him personally ("Anything that involved the word *star* always sounded like it was speaking directly to me"[13]). His chronicling of passions and remembered interactions make the novel a kind of puzzle that compels us to ruminate almost desperately over how he arrived where he is, a puzzle that remains largely intact even after that last page, and I don't believe I've even begun to crack it. But there's an exchange with his father I find extraordinarily evocative, profoundly heartbreaking and somehow triumphantly familiar. It's a memory from his teenage years in—you guessed it—the eighties.

Sean Phillips's father yells at the television. The yelling involves a requisite turning up of the volume, and this makes the family dinnertime a kind of hours-long insane asylum. In this instance, it's Muammar Gaddafi at whom Sean's father rages, and he tries to pull Sean in to no avail: "I couldn't make myself care much about it: it seemed like nothing; I couldn't keep any of it straight." Amid stories of gas prices, bites of meatloaf and Phillips telling his mother he likes the sauce, an overheard phrase gets him thinking: "American ships in Libyan water." At a commercial break, he tries to jump in.

"Dad, are Libyan waters different from other waters?"

His mother tries to discourage the conversation before it can begin, but his father responds, "They're different because of sovereignty."

"But there aren't any actual lines on the water or anything."

"They have maps and coordinates."

"Right, but the water—"

"The water is the same."

There is no dropping of the microphone, because this is where it ends. But in the narrative now, Phillips tells us how pleased he was to let the matter rest there "out in international waters with imaginary lines on their surface that no one could actually see."[14]

Take that, you mad, mad world. And may we all find in the gift a way in which to put such extraordinary moments of seeing, this alienated instance of true vision, this steadfast refusal of one tired old teleprompter. Perhaps the novel is one way. And there's also the way that overcomes estrangement whenever we put a truly open-ended question to someone else and truly wait quietly and expectantly for a response. When we manage that one—and there are friendly folks the world over who are managing it even now—we can know that the way of the gift is being embodied somewhere. It happens whenever we pay proper heed to one another in the giving and receiving of witness, whenever people *actually communicate* with one another. When that near-miraculous-feeling transaction occurs, perhaps it's appropriate to consider it an exemplary instance of true religion, the process whereby people experience themselves and their resources—their ancestors, too—as gifts.

When we think of it this way, religion is perhaps most helpfully conceived of as the question of what tales and traditions our lives embody. Everybody embodies *something*, after all. We're never not embodying. If religion is a concept we might begin to apply to ourselves with the same ease we project it upon others, it might even expand the horizon of personal honesty and help keep before ourselves the hope of being—or proving to have been—at least every so often true. Perhaps there are unexpected resources available to us in this lifelong work.

4

I learned it by watching you

A lifetime of conditioning could be overcome, but not easily.

Dana Franklin in Octavia Butler's *Kindred*

YOU CAN IMAGINE THE THRILL it is to me to teach—not just in my mind but to people in a classroom who occasionally write down the things I say—a course titled Religion and Science Fiction. Those two abstractions are, in some sense, the bookends of everything I'm excited about. Where else can we go to begin to see that the big ideas that make us miserable, jerking us around like mixed-up marionettes, decreeing that the way things are is the way they have to be, might be seen as nothing more than consensual fictions? And if they're only time-honored fictions, why don't we begin to withdraw our consent in small and maybe even occasionally big ways? What would happen then? Maybe we're at an amazing juncture full of unforeseen possibilities right now.

Money? A collective hallucination. Progress? For whom and according to what? Authority? That's an open question since what we call *authorized* is relative to what functions as a teleprompter in our lives, who it is we're willing to credit with magical powers of authorization, those *authors* of our fates to whom we anxiously look to be told what's permissible and even possible. Boundaries? Well, they've been drawn up over time, and they somehow stuck. Like all *design*ated areas, it's a question of design. Whose designations do we find necessary, healthy or even sacred? Everything depends upon our sacred designations: private property, sacraments, militarized zones, places of worship, border patrols. Are these design decisions eternal, sensible or even worthy? Science fiction addresses these questions by way of thought experiments. Throw people into the distant future and see what happens. Or hurl them backward into an inconceivably ancient past. Introduce technology that completely flips the script of what we think we know. Bring aliens into the equation and ask them about their standards for how to rightly measure intelligent life. Who's civilized *now*?

SCIENCE FICTION BREAKS THE ICE

Like nothing else can, science fiction invites us to take the temperature of our own strange behavior, to note the outrageous arbitrariness at work in our organizing fictions and to proceed more wonderingly in our conception of ourselves. It raises the question of how we've been imprinted. At its best, it performs nothing less than a prophetic and revivifying function in my own life. It makes me more alive to certain incongruities I've allowed to become somehow normalized. And as any lover of sci-fi understands implicitly, the contradictions were normalized *for* me long before I was born. Do I care to live up to that one *Star Trek* episode that got me thinking about all the subtle ways the Borg represents the strong forces of spirit-deadening conformity? Am I a red pill or a blue pill person?

Taking science fiction in—reading, watching and talking about it—is one of my favorite ways of doing battle with my own thoughtlessness. And against the caricature of the sci-fi enthusiast as a geek or a nerd who refuses to grow up, I'd like to somehow cling—for dear life—to the sense of play that comes easiest to us in childhood, while also arguing that the lover of sci-fi might best be seen as someone peculiarly determined to *keep* growing up and evolving, hunting down tales, analogies and even facts that serve to sharpen our sense of wonder at the weird worlds we're in. To begin to wonder, as Aristotle instructs us, is to begin to philosophize, and philosophy is bad news for bad religion. As I've come to see it, science fiction culture itself is a space in which to plot resistance to all the bad religion that shapes our thinking, asserting its pressure in our minds and nervous systems, narrowing our sense of what's possible, coloring our perceptions of people and events. I have in mind the phenomenon of *ideology*, which often appears to be the moving target at which my favorite science fiction takes aim.

Like brainwash, ideology isn't something anyone is likely to knowingly avow any more than we would think it kind to congratulate people for how thoroughly conformist they are. But the word is incredibly

> **Science fiction culture itself is a space in which to plot resistance to all the bad religion that shapes our thinking.**

useful in naming a creeping madness we're usually powerless to detect. Along these lines, William Pietz defines *ideological* as "how you have to *think* in order to *feel* morally good about yourself, given what you actually *do*."[1] Ideology is the supreme nut—the hardness of head and heart, the thickness of falsehood—that generations of prophets have sought to crack, the self-legitimating mind that can't afford (and won't be made) to think twice or to look again. What do we find ourselves thinking we *have* to think? How do we begin to overcome the pinched, defensive smile of *No further questions*?

Science fiction breaks the ice. Like any good parable, poem, film or song, it is a call to *keep thinking* when everyone else appears to have stopped. This might name the lonely virtue we honor—perhaps unintentionally—when we call someone a nerd. Science fiction almost tricks us into being nerds, spitting us out the end of a story only to discover we've succumbed to an insight we never signed up for. Momentarily deprived of our powers of prejudgment and presupposition, it catches us, like a good joke, with our defenses down. Rod Serling describes the process as a method he discovered gradually while composing vignettes of sometimes-alarming moral weirdness for *The Twilight Zone*: "I found it was all right to have Martians saying things Democrats and Republicans could never say."[2]

A SONG IS A MIND CRYING OUT

Consider the Doctor. I refer to the two-thousand-plus-year-old Gallifreyan, a Time Lord, who comes to us as the two-hearted protagonist of the *Doctor Who* series. In its fifty-year history, the question, "Doctor *who*?" has been wisely left unanswered. As a character conveniently capable of regeneration, he's been played by fourteen different actors, at last count, each of whom crafts a being who is a lives-long learner whose fiercely intelligent love for the human race spans space and time. Whatever the planet or historical period his time-traveling spacecraft the TARDIS (Time And Relative Dimensions in Space) gets him to, he sizes up the scene with a moral and intellectual rigor that upsets the dehumanizing status quo of the day. Ever alive to what everyone else has yet to notice, the Doctor doesn't ultimately *miss* people, and he can pull what is interesting out of anything and anyone. As our best nerd, he often seems hell-bent on persuading his friends and companions to be *better* nerds, to find themselves more interesting, to live up to the complexity of what's before them, to somehow rise above their conditioning.

That call to think again and more and further, to be born again once again through the renewal of the mind, is a call the Doctor also heeds himself as it's sounded by friends, alleged enemies and those he might be tempted to view as lower life forms. An especially telling instance in which the actor David Tennant's Doctor gets schooled for his inattentiveness occurs in an episode called "Planet of the Ood." Having once encountered the Ood as the cheerfully docile servants of humans in the forty-second century, he presumes that they are what their minders conceived and acquired them as, creatures too simple minded to desire or dream of anything more than their current lot in life: "Born to serve." Regarded as something akin to well-trained, "mildly telepathic" pets with human-like bodies, communicative devices tied to their anatomy and faces that look like especially worrying seafood, he'd had yet to delve into the prickly question of labor relations.

Everything changes when the Doctor and his companion, Donna Noble, a present-day Londoner who has left her temp work to see what traveling in the TARDIS might yield, hear a song which leads them to an escaped Ood bleeding to death from bullet wounds. The Doctor had experienced the Ood as servers bringing food and drink and offering various forms of assistance, but now he's heard one calling out to him telepathically. "That was the song," he explains. "It was his mind crying out." With the help of a map alleged to chart Ood Operations, they begin to see that distribution centers lead to processing plants and eventually make their way to a restricted warehouse in which the Ood are kept in containers. Having been initially wowed by the technological advances and the intergalactic distances traveled by her forty-second-century descendants, Donna is disgusted and appalled: "A great big empire built on slavery."

"It's not so different from your time," the Doctor observes.

"Oy!" she exclaims. "I haven't got slaves."

"Who do you think made your clothes?"

I'm loathe to risk spoiling this tale by saying much more, but there's an especially telling exchange when the Doctor and Donna try to enlist the help of Solana Mercurio, the charming and clever head of public relations for Ood Operations. Might she be persuaded to blow the whistle? If the people of Earth knew what was being done to the Ood, Donna reasons, they wouldn't stand for it.

"Oh, don't be so stupid," Solana exclaims. "Of course they know." How can that be? "They don't ask. Same thing."

The Doctor weighs in: "Solana, the Ood aren't born like this. They can't be. A species born to serve could never evolve in the first place. What does the company do to make them obey?"

"That's nothing to do with me."

"Oh, what, because you don't *ask*?" As ever, the Doctor never stops trying to pull us out of whatever trance we're in, whatever bits of observable reality we've kept isolated from one another as if to purposefully avoid the moral realization that could change everything for the better. Over a millennium or so of observation, he's seen his share of ideology and all the ways we have of misnaming progress, civilization and development. The era and the alien species might differ, but the groupthink remains the same. He falls into it himself from time to time: "Last time I met the Ood, I never thought. I never asked . . . I didn't need the map. I should have *listened*."

The Doctor admonishes himself once more to learn and act upon a literacy of wonder, that habit of attentiveness that is obviously a moral and a political literacy as well. In episode after episode, he shows us what a bearer of extraordinary consciousness looks like while also offering hints and indications of how ours might be extraordinary too. Like his companions, we're all one moment of concentration away from seeing some crucial something we had yet to let ourselves see. We'll have to widen our horizon of expectation if we're to really see and listen and wake up to the mess we're in *and* all the strange and beautiful ways we might yet turn the world around.

THE THINGS YOU MAKE UP . . . THE RULES

The Doctor invites us to gaze upon one another as if we were all fantastic beings—because every day is an opportunity to learn again that we are. He also exemplifies the manner in which good humor, compassion and a well-chosen word can occasionally overcome blind power. Admonished to dwell no longer in unawareness concerning our own weird surroundings (Who built this? What holds these people in awe? What are they afraid of? What leaps of faith were taken and why?), the Doctor enthusiast asks what's normal and why, or more specifically, what's been *normalized* from on high and why it all went that way.

And what goes for the Whovian goes for anyone with a hole in the heart that can only be filled by science fiction. So when it comes to my fellow sci-fiers, how do I urge upon them my stop-pretending-you're-not-religious campaign? Generally they're already up for this kind of thing because they're desperately eager to flip the given script. The *received* religion—which is the *reigning* religion—won't do. Uncritical subservience is, as ever, the problem.

In my experience, lovers of science fiction don't read or tune in to stories in the sad and simple hope of having their own ideas about life reinforced. Driven by their own curiosity, they are *eager* to immerse themselves in strange new worlds where their customary paradigms stop working and they feel the need to grapple their way toward better ones, to dream further and more deeply. Like the Doctor, they know there's always more out there to think through, more realizations of complexity to be had, more that would show us how our reigning conceptions turn out to be woefully arbitrary and insufficient. As the Time Lord himself (the Peter Capaldi iteration) puts it: "I believe I haven't seen everything. I don't know. It's funny, isn't it? The things you make up—*the rules*. . . . Still, that's why I keep travelling. To be proved wrong."

These words witness to the desire to always try to see what we're not seeing, the determination to be ever wary of our own peculiar habits of inattentiveness. The Doctor comes to learn, again and again, that this is the only chance of ever really seeing or understanding who and what's in front of our noses. In a two-part episode ("Hungry Earth"/"Cold Blood"), Matt Smith's Doctor leads the charge of widening consciousness when he discovers, together with his companions Amy Pond and Rory Williams, that a drilling operation in Wales is about to ignite a war between humanity and an ancient species hibernating deep within the Earth.

SOMEHOW MAKE IT KNOWN

Nasreen Chaudhry, the lead scientist in charge of the drilling, and a local family are in panic over the sudden appearance of sinkholes and masked figures with hostile intentions. But the Doctor has determined that they're experiencing the bio-programmed response of Earth's original inhabitants, the Silurians, who descended to subterranean depths twenty million years ago in anticipation of the catastrophic collision which proved to be nothing more than the moon aligning with the Earth. The "prehistoric" trace minerals Silurian scientists purposefully engineered to appear in the blue grass unique to the area as a word of caution ("Do not disturb") have been misperceived by Chaudhry and her backers as a scientifically interesting "X marks the spot," signifying "Drill, baby, drill." There's a disaster waiting to happen.

As the locals begin to arm themselves against sure retaliation, the Doctor has his work cut out for him: "No, no weapons. It's not the way I do things. . . . You're better than this. I'm asking nicely. Put them away." But for most Homo sapiens, the sight of angry, unreasoning lizard people overwhelms the Doctor's well-reasoned pleas that they're about to miss the historic opportunity to be their most decent, brilliant and inspiring selves in their first encounter with Homo reptilia. Does he really think one can negotiate with these aliens? "They're *not* aliens," he insists. "They're Earth-liens. . . . The previous owners of the planet, that's all. Look, from their point of view, you're the invaders. *Your* drill was threatening *their* settlement."

And sure enough, we come to find out that Silurian culture has within it an almost even match when it comes to fear, defensiveness and a tendency to demonize the unfamiliar. Silurians too have bellicose leaders who mistake empathy for weakness, who proudly refuse to negotiate with apes and who deem us, given our track record of ecological destruction with no thought for the morrow, "a vermin race." Violence escalates, but cooler heads on both sides of the genetic divide become ambassadors for their species, together concluding that while a *genuinely shared* Earth is their only hope, the people of the Earth need more time. (Chaudhry: "Nobody on the surface is going to go for this idea. It is just too big a leap.") As much as they wish we'd all been ready for the revelation of intelligent life above and below and all the ways we'll have to change our ways of thinking and living, humanity isn't ready yet.

"But maybe it should be," the Doctor decrees, and his solution will involve folklore, hibernation and asking all parties to bank everything on the hope—what else is there?—of future harmony. "So, here's a deal. Everybody listening. . . . Activate shutdown. I'll amend the system, set your alarm for a thousand years' time. A thousand years to sort the planet out. *To be ready.* Pass it on. As legend or prophecy or religion, but *somehow make it known*: This planet is to be shared." The shared vision of a shared world will have to be learned *by heart,* a transaction carried over and somehow seen through one changed mind at a time. Everything depends upon this ethical summons, this sacred intuition, this *ancient know-how* handed down. Perhaps future generations will know what to make of it, how to take care within the legacy that is their own livelihood. Then and now and later, the available lore is an appeal to our wits, the literature that is a kind of Early Warning System. The good religion the Doctor proposes be set in motion *one more time* is that story and song through which human coherence, figurative and literal, is passed down to others as tradition, as a living possibility.

There will remain a vision for the appointed time. Such a song, should it in any sense remain the same, can serve as a vessel of unbroken solidarity. As redemption songs do, it infiltrates our thinking, lyrically signaling the fact of kindred spirits who once articulated a hoped-for righteousness that might yet register one fine day. According to this familiar trope, the wisdom of ancient traditions is nothing less than the carefully cultivated, long-haul awareness of those who precede us, once ancient but now contemporary if anyone out there has an ear to hear and an eye to see. This is tradition as G. K. Chesterton conceives it, as the democracy of the dead. It turns out that those imaginative, long-suffering, long-dead people who saw fit to preserve, copy and write so many things down often knew exactly what they were on about. Might we yet receive their good sense? Can they get a witness in the here and now?

AN ETHIC IS A WAY OF THINKING

To really receive a witness—to bear, embody, give and pass it on—is a very different matter from making a purchase, acquiring information or absent-mindedly downloading a song. Witness calls for *with*ness, the complete opposite of detached observation. It's getting in on someone else's act. It's a live grappling that gives way to a realization that *this* has to do with *that*. A realization, we understand, can't be force-fed on a person or a people, but it can be taken up and lived up to, not as a possession but as an experience. To receive the witness of another is to enter into a vision that isn't accessible to us in isolation; we realize ourselves as members of one another and feel compelled to act accordingly, finding that we can't easily *live with ourselves* if we don't.

> **To receive the witness of another is to enter into a vision that isn't accessible to us in isolation.**

One of the best illustrations I know of when it comes to communicating a sacred call to revere ourselves and others comes from Theodore Sturgeon and his classically weird and wonderful 1953 sci-fi novel *More Than Human*. As Sturgeon's story goes, the next stage in human evolution doesn't come as one gifted individual arising among Homo sapiens but as a small group of uniquely gifted individuals who are deficient to the point of incapacity apart from access to the gifts of one another. One's a telepath, another can practice telekinesis, a couple have powers of teleportation and one, referred to as Baby, has boundless mental capacities that can only be communicated and experienced by way of the other four. Taken together, they form *Homo Gestalt*. They function together through a process called—wait for it—*bleshing*. And when they blesh, there's almost nothing they can't do.

As *Homo Gestalt* find each other the story addresses the question of what they believe they're to do with themselves, what they *want* to do given the amazing facts of what they *can* do. "Can something be more important than anything else in the world, and you can't even remember what it is?" asks the one.

"It happens," answers the other.

"It's happened to me," the one observes. "I don't like it either."[3]

Questions of how to relate, how to behave and what might be essential to continued evolution are at the heart of the novel, which amounts to an illuminating meditation on how to know how to live. Sturgeon: "Morals are an obedience to rules that people laid down to help you live among them."[4] Or as one member of *Homo Gestalt* puts it to another, "An ethic isn't a fact you can look up. It's a way of thinking."[5]

Like the rest of us (and this is why I turn to Sturgeon repeatedly), they'll have to learn to ease up, to hold things dear and to resist proceeding through our world in a clenched-fist fashion; it's a life's work, or the work of many lives over time, to be sure. Joy won't be accessed through haste, fear or anger. Like so much science fiction, *More Than Human* is a surprising and provocative tale of misapprehension that is also an evocative, enigmatic trail of crumbs toward *right* apprehension. Whatever the genre or the form, we get to collect whatever vision might serve as one more apocalypse, endlessly applicable to so many of our own immediate quandaries, one more bright electric avenue to new and better ways of conceiving ourselves and others. We don't just get to; we *have* to. It's how we all go about getting by. Or trying to.

To Be Whole Is to Be Part

If you want to make it back home you have to keep moving forward, consenting—again and again—to being transformed by the renewing of your mind, to learning, revising and resisting once more the bad habit of mistaking your sense of reality for reality itself. You have to let the sweet old world, the faces of others and their words, the minute particulars of your own existence mean more than they did the day before. You have to see it all again, to *re*spect and *re*consider, thinking repentantly by thinking again, because revolution begins with the thinking mind.

The preceding three sentences are my attempted mash-up of more voices than my consciousness knows to credit. But I do have a couple firmly in mind. One is the apostle Paul's exhorting the church in Rome to resist, in view of the living mercy of God, the easy conformity to the reigning thought habits of the at-large world and the haughtiness of thought we often adopt to somehow legitimize ourselves over against others. The other is the intuition of a woman named Laia Asieo Odo, a character created by Ursula K. Le Guin, who describes her as "one of the ones who walked away from Omelas."[6]

"To be whole is to be part; true journey is return,"[7] Odo likes to say. And her way of putting things always draws from a persistently righteous vision of social cohesion and, almost synonymously for Odo, human pleasure: "It is useless work that darkens the heart. The delight of the nursing mother, of the scholar, of the successful hunter, of the good cook, of the skilful maker, of anyone doing needed work and doing it well—this durable joy is perhaps the deepest source of human affection, and of sociality as a whole." This anthropological premise—perhaps you can feel it coming—gives rise to an entire philosophy of life well lived and, as you might guess, a word or two on the right rearing of children. A young person unversed in the pressures of profiteering and the maddening misperception that is private property "will grow up with the will to do what needs doing and the capacity for joy in doing it."[8]

The witness of Odo hits its stride, in Le Guin's fiction, a few generations after her death in the form of Odonianism, a revolutionary movement whose adherents are peppered across the nations of the planet Urras. Fearing overthrow, each nation accords the Odonians the rights of noninterference and permission to settle Urras's neighboring habitable moon, Anarres. This is the setup of Le Guin's novel *The Dispossessed*, which follows the life of a physicist named Shevek who will strive to live up to the Odonian vision within—and in spite of—an often only nominally Odonian society now 200 years into its settlement on Anarres. From the outset, it's the tale of this one Odonian's slow return (true journey *is* return) to Urras in pursuit of his vocation, but it's also the chronicling of Shevek's own voyage of discovery concerning what constitutes true movement and the development of his own ever-burgeoning literacy of wonder.

While his interest in physics will eventually land him elsewhere, the young Shevek we meet early in the novel finds durable joy elusive, and his mood is relentlessly darkened by labor that strikes him as completely useless. Labor in the Settlement of Anarres is conducted within co-ops, and he first begins to move outside his peer groups in an afforestation project, in which thousands of settlers attempt to replant a forest lost over millennia to drought. Exhausted and covered in dust like everyone else, he grows exasperated one evening when a female coworker, Gimar, sings for the thousandth time a lyric about an enigmatic "she" who somehow brings forth "green leaf from the stone" and from the rock's heart "clear water running."

"Who does?" Shevek demands. "Who's 'she'?"

"It's a miners song."

"Well, then, who's 'she'?"

"I don't know," Gimar observes, befuddled. "It's just what the song says. Isn't it what we're doing here? Bringing green leaves out of stones!"

"Sounds like religion."

"You and your fancy book-words. It's just a song."[9]

In exchanges like these, Shevek is constantly challenged to stop mistaking his preferred abstractions for reality and to see, hear and feel what's really in front of him. It's a life's work for all of us, but he'll have to fight the mind-deadening pressure to live life at the mercy of other people's generalizations. In that place where Shevek is apt to congratulate himself for having successfully sniffed out "religion" [slow clap], Gimar hears instead—and sings—a poetics that might yet take form, that indeed *has* taken form in the very work they're up to. She hears nothing less than a sweet record of struggle—and the taking of courage *despite* the struggle—resonating wonderfully with their own.

To call it mere fantasy or fairy tale or, in the tired old pejorative sense, religion, is a sad and snippy diminishment of possibility. It's also to restrict unnecessarily our realization of the organic fact of other people and the accompanying sense of solidarity none of us can live without. Every song, we get to understand, is potentially a song of myself, a song of yourself and of many other selves. What was real and of value to our ancestors might make it down to us. In a meaningful measure, we *can* have what they had. It can survive in us and, when it does, we're afforded a renewed sense of orientation, a way in the wilderness where once, in our reluctance to credit much of anything or anyone, it appeared there was no way out or through.

Gimar will urge upon Shevek that more excellent way of the open hand. He will learn the life-giving trick of loving the world without looking down on it and revering life in all of its manifestations. Like others before him, he'll take up the wonderful habit of seeing the mythic in the allegedly trivial, a sacred drama at work in the faces of those who cross his path and an apocalypse in the everyday. To see an image evoked by something else is to have received a sign, and it happens all the time. The least we can do is try to observe consciously what's been given to us to know. We will inevitably miss so much, but we don't have to miss it all. We can be among those who insist on being awake to their own experience. It is fitting and helpful to refer to these social collectives as sacred traditions available and hospitable to us even in our fevered now. Access to poetic intuition, a revelatory understanding of the situations vouchsafed unto us, might be nearer than we're prone to guess. The connective tissue we require might be within reach, one lyric, Scripture, song or dance away.

Disinformation Is Noise Posing as Signal

We know our own desperate need in this regard and how easily we're drawn into the high-tech schemes that mean to profit from our carefully cultivated confusion, our isolation and our escalating defensiveness. We need not look terribly far to see, *to feelingly perceive*, that it takes a village to perceive a reality. In this too science fiction goes ever before us. And the advance scout to whom I owe so much is an apostle of misapprehension sometimes referred to as the Shakespeare of science fiction: Philip Kindred Dick.

"Reality is that which, when you stop believing in it, doesn't go away," Dick famously observed.[10] And for all the black humor one might sense in an adage like that one, it's the kind of reminder Dick was committed to placing before himself. In his sensitive, funny and often heartbreaking view of the world, we all keep faith with one flawed but sincere vision of things or another, and all community is *faith-based* community. What we're left with is good faith, bad faith and an ever-proliferating inventory of disinformation, an ocean of noise on which it can seem all but impossible to discern a single human voice. Whether badly or beautifully, all of Dick's characters are engaged in the modest and universal struggle of trying to make sense, of trying to *be significant* to somebody somewhere somehow.

Those who take on this task are met with certain difficulties in a world where disinformation drives the popular economy and is therefore made to be practically omnipresent and new every morning. (All proselytization. All the time.) Disinformation is the noise that drives out true significance. And worse, it is noise *posing as* significance. Or in Dick's phrase, "It is noise posing as signal so you do not even recognize it as noise." His take on the sad situation includes a word of warning concerning the injury the powers that be *themselves* sustain: "If you can float enough disinformation into circulation you will totally abolish everyone's contact with reality, probably your own included."[11]

Every Dick novel offers countless scenarios so eye-rubbingly pre-scient (appliances turned companions, commercials physically accompanying you through your days and nights, corporate seizure of natural resources, people lost in their hopeless little screens) that you can find yourself checking and double-checking publishing dates. In 1965, for instance, he gave us *The Three Stigmata of Palmer Eldritch*, which features an Earth so cooked that a person can't go outside in the daytime without a body-cooling apparatus (Antarctica excepted, at least for now). But having sold the atmosphere to the highest bidders over time, the governments of the nations of Earth have come together to colonize what habitable planets they can find to ensure that their citizens remain profitably in motion on the treadmills of that one world religion too ubiquitous to even question: global consumerism. Enter Perky Pat Layouts.

Shared Faith and Bad Thinking

The situation with Perky Pat Layouts is almost too strange to conceive until you come to see it as a kind of proto-online network. It's as if Dick had a vision of the Internet but could only cobble an idea together with the materials at hand. Perky Pat Layouts (P. P. Layouts, Inc., based in New York City) are a hot commodity among the sad, displaced citizens-turned-colonists for whom our world is now a distant memory. With the aid of a drug called Can-D, they're left to gather in windswept hovels on arid, mostly inhospitable planets to stare at their P. P. Layouts—and they really are *layouts*, mere props involving dolls, cars, houses, electric garage doors and all manner of miniature artifacts of a culture no longer available to them— imagining and hallucinating together in a desperate frenzy of pseudo-intimacy. It's a dystopian take akin to an age in which humans will abide anything so long as they have free Wi-Fi.

Seeking transit, they call it. And who among us doesn't hope to do just that? Leave it to Dick to submit for our approval a meditation on the variations of *shared faith* that make for our every shot at social cohesion or, to put it old school, communion. Every P. P. Layout customer enters in responding to the promise of momentary transcendence, but the levels of expectation differ as well as the theories and testimonies concerning what precisely they are experiencing. Here's Dick on one hopeful soul named Sam Regan:

> He himself was a believer; he affirmed the miracle of translation—the near-sacred moment in which the miniature

artifacts of the layout no longer merely represented Earth but *became* Earth. And he and the others, joined together in the fusion of doll-inhabitation by means of the Can-D, were transported outside of time and local space. Many of the colonists were as yet unbelievers; to them the layouts were merely symbols of a world which none of them could any longer experience. But one by one, the unbelievers came around.

As is the case for the other colonists, Regan finds that the hope for that little bit of human-like touch haunts him like a muscle memory every moment of every day. "Even now . . . he yearned to go back down below, chew a slice of Can-D from his hoard, and join with his fellows in the most solemn moment of which they were capable."[12]

One of the joys of reading Dick is the constant rediscovery that the tone with which he delivers assessments like these ("the most solemn moment of which they were capable") is anything but derisive. While we're right to find ourselves rooting for those few colonists who manage to resist the allure of Perky Pat and Can-D, those rare birds who are committed to somehow living inside their own bodies and, in spite of their lost world, trying to cultivate, plant and harvest alien lands, Dick won't let us feel complete contempt for those who lose their way, because he never lets us forget that we *are* they. We are these sad, beautiful, well-meaning people. His refusal to resort to parody or condescension renders his analysis of all the wearying behaviors humans get used to—that we settle for and even come to revel in—all the more incisive.

This question of what gets normalized, the mad, bad ideas that keep us crazy, destructive and horribly unaware of ourselves in cycles of soul-deadening conformity, is the very question science fiction keeps constantly in play. And insofar as it serves us in this way, I think it is a sort of sacred genre. Science fiction is where we

get to hold a colloquy with our own bad thinking, staging a feud
with the status quo, puncturing the perverse visions that pass for
normal one strange tale at a time. It cultivates within its audience
a certain lyrical aliveness to the reigning dysfunction of our worlds
and an awareness articulate enough to call that dysfunction more
constantly into question.

Lifetimes of Conditioning

No novel I can think of delivers on this promise quite so powerfully and disturbingly as Octavia Butler's *Kindred*, the tale of Dana,
a black female writer in modern-day California who finds herself
suddenly and inexplicably pulled back in time to save a drowning
child, the son of a plantation owner in pre–Civil War Maryland.
It isn't a dream, and it occurs repeatedly and unexpectedly
throughout the child Rufus's growing-up years, whenever his life's
in jeopardy at various stages of his nineteenth-century existence.
Mere days can pass in Dana's time when she's suddenly dragged
into the path of Rufus, who may have aged in months or years
while she's been away, and her return to her own time can occur
just as randomly. "I don't have a name for the thing that happened
to me," she explains to her bewildered but believing husband, "but
I don't feel safe any more."[13]

The issue of her natural compulsion to save Rufus again and again
is, of course, complicated, as is her hope that she might somehow
enlighten and educate him enough to improve her own chances of
survival as well as that of others like her—but also *not* like her—who
have been consigned to lives of slavery. How can she persuade Rufus
to rise above the perverse imagination of his people? Dana has no
illusions concerning what she's up against: "A lifetime of conditioning
could be overcome, but not easily."[14] And what will become of her
own conscience as she restrains her vision of what could and should
be, keeping quiet about it in order to stay alive?

Amazingly, her contemplation of her upside-down situation includes an expression of qualified sympathy for Rufus's father, Tom, who according to the present arrangement owns her. "His father wasn't the monster he could have been with the power he held over his slaves. He wasn't a monster at all. Just an ordinary man who sometimes did the monstrous things his society said were legal and proper."[15] There is so much to weigh out in these remarkable words, in the way Dana can credit a terrorist with a degree of decency given the social dictates of his time, and in the tyranny of normalcy at work in the hearts of both victims and executioners. She will bank everything on the hope of bringing a light of revolutionary awareness to a murderously brutal age. Her tale can hardly be said to contain a resolution but, like a good parable, it offers itself as a cause for moral reflection and a profound vision of how the past impinges on the present, despite whatever psychosis of denial and forgetting we bring to our conceptions of history.

When I read *Kindred* with students, we're constantly confronted by the notion that the life you live will keep on being the life you're able to realize, the vision of being with yourself and others you've *learned*, for better or worse, *by heart*. "I learned it by watching you!" cries the son to the father in the old anti-drug PSA. And the preachiness of the scene now functions as a kind of pop-culture truism on the inevitability of influence, the pull of learned behavior, the way we can hardly see past what's been normalized for each of us in our lifetimes of cultural immersion.

The overwhelming difficulty of breaking these cycles, of awakening to ourselves and of somehow renewing our tired minds toward transformation is not a recent development in human affairs. In one of Jesus' strangest and most challenging sayings, he advises his hearers that fullness of life under the reign of God comes down largely to a question of vision. When the eye, being the lamp of the body, is healthy, your whole body is full of light.

When it's impaired? Darkness. Seemingly straightforward enough, but we would be wrong to think the teaching could ever end so unparadoxically. The zinger: "See to it, then, that the light within you is not darkness." (Luke 11:35).

Try *that*. Might something be amiss in our imagination from time to time? Oh my goodness, yes. So much so that we're often prone to mistake darkness for light and vice versa. Make sure that what you take to be light within you isn't actually darkness. We can, as it turns out, get that wrong. And unlearning the reigning dysfunction we unwittingly inherit and obey isn't something we can pull off overnight. It's an unlearning we're never done doing, because righteousness is endlessly complicated. We're never done seeking it out. We have to have our minds renewed and our thinking transformed continuously like children. We get to be born again and again and again.

5

Hurry up and matter!

*Sometimes I look at people and I make myself
try and feel them as more than just
a random person walking by.*

**Joaquin Phoenix's Theodore Twombly
in Spike Jonze's *Her***

NEW BIRTH. HOW MIGHT WE GO ABOUT getting started on that one?
Does it feel like it's somehow already too late? Is it a possibility we often suspect we can't even afford to get into? Is it all too complicated? How did this come to be?

Have a look at this:

A multitude of causes, unknown to former times, are now acting with a combined force to blunt the discriminating powers of the mind, and unfitting it for all voluntary exertion to reduce it to a state of almost savage torpor. The most effective of these causes are the great national events which are daily taking place, and the increasing accumulation of men in cities, where the uniformity of their occupations produces a craving for extraordinary incident, which the rapid communication of intelligence hourly gratifies. . . . When I think upon this degrading thirst after outrageous stimulation, I am almost ashamed to have spoken of the feeble effort with which I have endeavored to defeat it.[1]

These are the remarkable words of one man determined to somehow rage against the machinery of mass hypnosis, the general hijacking of the human imagination, and the way we have of fearfully sealing ourselves off from one another in informational echo chambers on account of a misconceived, self-degrading thirst for stimulation. We might find it heartening to note that this description of a crisis "unknown to former times" was published a decade or so before "The Star-Spangled Banner." The lone resister who penned them is William Wordsworth, and the feeble effort he's undertaken to defeat this degradation of human spirit, and of which he says he's almost ashamed to have spoken at all given the apparent futility of the situation, is his own modest word-work. It's poetry he's up to, and he defines it a little famously in this same essay—a preface actually—as "the spontaneous overflow of powerful feeling."

Poetry isn't popularly posited these days as the corrective to our perpetual disquieting or as a habit of mind by which we might get ahold of ourselves. Upon being handed a volume of poetry, probably no one has ever experienced the following message:

"What's this?"

"I'm glad you asked. It's a space from which to challenge the reigning distortions of your everyday life."

"Could you be more specific?"

"With pleasure. It's another person's enlivening testimony, their deep-diving so to speak, on your behalf and mine. It's liable to strike a righteous chord. It might also again awaken you to the fact that you live on a planet, that you need not dwell so damagingly upon it and that the natural world is on your side. It's not an environment after all. It's a neighborhood. You're here to enjoy yourself sensually—to experience yourself—as a gift and in the gift of other people. And the expressions collected in these pages—here, hand it back and I'll read one aloud in a moment—we call poetry, our best word for that which makes things new, that which [whispering] aids us in holding everything dear. It's [louder] the spontaneous overflow of powerful feeling [quieter] that takes its origin from emotion recollected in tranquility."

Poetry is at least that. It's a form of behavior, too. I can even think of people I'd say have been kind enough to *treat* me poetically. A teacher listened to me explain what I thought a passage in a novel was getting at and fixed me with a look that said, "I just know you can do better than that." A librarian looked at my account and said, "David Dark. Now that's a writer's name." And a woman in Dublin who'd agreed to house a friend and me for a few nights looked at me a second or two longer than I was accustomed to as I crossed her threshold and said with warm solemnity, "You're welcome." Poetry happens when I'm made to really see something I've overlooked, something needful, something that might bring me back to myself. I can say of so many things, "That was poetry to me."

And oh how we need it if we're to ever be true, if we're to be witnesses to our own existence. Seeing that he only had newsprint to contend with (though the steam locomotive was right around the corner), we can easily conclude that Wordsworth had it rather easy when it comes to self-presence, hearing your own voice and trying to know where you are and what you're about. If the rush of getting and spending in his own day had him feeling that the mass of humanity was out of tune, unmoved and slowly frittering their souls away with worldly care, we can only imagine what he'd make of the endless distraction available to the Western world today in the ubiquitous form of our electronic devices and the accompanying difficulties of discernment in a frenzied age of everything all of the time. For many of us, it's as if we're witnessing the steady erosion of our ability to have face-to-face conversation, to allow ourselves the luxury of sustained attention to another person's words, to know the sacred pleasure of nuance.

HIGH-TECH HASTE

The prophet of the technological bluff, Jacques Ellul, could not have foreseen the days when agitated people would gaze plaintively into someone's eyes and ask, "Do you have Internet?" But he demonstrated profound prescience when he observed that a computer isn't a companion; it's a vampire.[2] I know it when I try to read a poem aloud to my students, asking them to let my voice address them in an absence of screens. It's as if I've deprived them of an essential form of sustenance. Drawing on Ellul's image and the Baptist activist-philosopher's term for televangelists, I sometimes offer a vision of what we're dealing with in these moments by observing aloud that cell phones might be instructively referred to as electric soul molesters.

Their bafflement at the proposal—and it only intensifies each year—is such that I could be running the risk of this being the only thing they remember about my class. But I also think it's very much worth it to get a form of systemic dysfunction unique to our age somehow on the table. Unfailingly and in brave new ways each time, we have a conversation I have yet to find a better way to begin. "Why do you call it that?" a student asked in wide-eyed and genuine exasperation one year. I'm intensely grateful for the voicing of this wonderfully direct question that called out the response that eventually came to me: Because it has a way of robbing *you* of our presence and robbing *us* of yours. They get it. The question of presence remains in play from there on out. What can we do about it? How are we to be true to one another in real time when the siren song is always right there, on your person, one buzz away?

There's a time to be on high alert for that one call, certainly, but what if we never aren't? If being true is being present to ourselves and our surroundings, what becomes of our truth-sensing faculties in a culture where people self-interrupt, on the average, every three minutes?[3] I would argue that our unwillingness to silence our phones often amounts to an effective silencing of our own insight as we edge out of our imaginations the time required to actually experience it. The same goes for the attention we expend checking in on our screens to see if we've heard back on that one thing. Largely estranged from our own intuition, it's as if our attention is stretched so thin and in so many different directions that we find ourselves deprived of the time and space in which to feel deeply and to form our own thoughts. Whether by way of advertising campaigns, the million-dollar messaging of campaign funders and their politico pretend public servant proxies, or the endless impinging of one more text message, our ability to see and think clearly can be constantly compromised by an endless diversion from the heart of any matter. As a serial tweeter myself, let it be known that this sermon comes self-administered.

Here again, when it's driven by a kind of high-tech haste, our innate desire to be social, a desire I take to be sacred in its way, gets preyed upon, and we find ourselves drowning in schemes that seem to have been purposefully designed to make us feel endlessly inadequate and largely powerless. In a wide variety of media, mechanisms of quick and easy gratification are catered and calibrated to play to our fantasies of ourselves even as they leave us dispirited, diminished and further estranged from the possibility of true, noncommercialized human interaction. Media companies' stock values soar, but we're left with what Stephen King refers to as a "catastrophically fragmented society"[4] in which everyone dreams their dreams alone, often in the darkness of issue silos and increasingly tragically unversed in the mental habits that might make for lived community.

"Every human being is involved in a desperate attempt to narrate himself into a safe place,"[5] novelist Richard Powers once remarked. And what a multiedged and variously cued dance the social pipeline is. "What's the story here?" we're in so many ways never *not* asking. How do I get *in*? Or alternately, how I do I get *out* of this horrible story? By narrating and *re*narrating away. What is the shape my devotion will take today? Will it be the sad tale my yesterday told? Cleansing breath. Focus. What's that voice saying as I reach again for the fire hose of Internet one more futile time? *Hurry up and matter!*

Call it an exorcism, if you'd like, or a poetic intervention or one more witticism by which we can have mercy on ourselves. But "Hurry up and matter," a phrase my poet-sage-lady-friend, partner in crime and matrimony, Sarah Masen, once offered aloud, has become a saving, clarifying mantra in our household. We have to give voice to the spirit that drives us nuts before we can dismiss it, effectively renounce it or say, "Get behind me, accuser!" We have many such phrases in our family's attention collection, our everyday liturgy. When I open up my laptop, for instance, she'll occasionally mock me, asking in a child's voice, "Did somebody write me?" Every so often, somebody I really ought to write back right about then *has* written me (or typed me), but the mockery is nevertheless a saving ministry. What am I trying to save myself from when I dip my head again in that current, and where am I hoping to get to? Am I rushing off to *feel* more relevant than the human beings nearby can make me feel? Fleeing the presence of my own presence in a rock-and-roll fantasy? "Hurry up and matter" often seems to name the age, our experience of it anyway, like nothing else. What better phrase is there to name the driving need—or *perceived* need—that takes me straight into the fuel tank of someone else's marketing scheme, away from where I actually am to some deluded, disembodied elsewhere?

GENUINE CONSCIOUSNESS VS. TRIVIALIZING SHALLOWNESS

This returns us to the question of what we're up to with our imaginations. And as ever, it isn't a *side* issue, because there are no sidelines. What I'm up to with my imagination *is* what I'm up to. It's me *making do.* And complicatedly—oh so complicatedly—neutrality doesn't appear to be a live option, because writer Ronald Sukenick was right: "If you don't use your own imagination, somebody else is going to use it for you."[6] The question of how I imagine myself and others is at the core of my lived life, how I relate (no getting away from relating), the way I dwell in the world. How shall I go about mattering if *not* mattering isn't an option for anyone anywhere anytime?

Slowly and carefully and with a wary eye on all the flashy, artificial offerings that serve to obscure the reality of where I'm sitting, standing or walking. There is so much that can call me away from a proper estimation of who I am, where I am and what the joys of right relation might yet require of me; so much that draws me into a denial of the reality of my own body, so much that drives me to deny, to my everlasting detriment and that of others, the fact of the living world. As I see it, we most effectively practice the right of dissent and resistance when we begin to realize that we're in the thick of a religious quandary, one in which we're in danger of no longer meaningfully experiencing our own lives. It's as if we're awash in bad ideas that often render us unable to engage with anything larger than our own misperceived egos. Recognizing bad religion when we see it—and it *is* coming at us from every angle—can make us more vigilant and alive to the possibilities of genuine consciousness and more wary of the trivializing shallowness into which we're otherwise unwittingly enlisted. Amid the

> **How might we access wisdom, compassion, hospitality and other forms of life for which there is no app?**

static that degrades, how might we access wisdom, compassion, hospitality and other forms of life for which there is no app?

As I see the bad religion situation, the answer isn't a matter of stepping out and starting new traditions so much as it's a matter of approaching the currents we're already in from a different angle, one person, one relationship at a time. And even putting it this way brings to mind the poet-pastor Eugene Peterson, who once observed that the besetting sin of the American people is probably impatience. This sounds so right to me, especially when I consider the possibility that there's hardly a sin I can think of that isn't somehow born of misperceived need, of haste and its accompanying inattentiveness, of some feverish variation once more of *Hurry up and matter!* Being true—*ringing* true—will have to involve a slow work of recognition and resistance to that mad and nervy, deluding spirit. To begin to be true is to try to choose—or *risk* choosing—presence over progress, *really* showing up and taking the time to wonder what we're really up to, what we're doing and why.

COURTESY OF THE HEART

It will require, in all things, what the poet William Stafford refers to as "courtesy of the heart." He purloins the phrase from Nietzsche as a way of elaborating on the necessity of attentiveness to the minute particulars, the little things, and a statement he overheard from a peer he knew in the Civilian Public Service: "I feel that if struck I should give off a clear note where I am. But I don't have to go around beating myself like a gong." Who we are, Stafford understands, will always be enmeshed in the particularities of what we do—and don't do. We owe it to one another—and ourselves—to be as absolutely honest as we can, to give off, as much as we are able, a clear note:

It's a kind of feeling of wanting to ride the contours of human relations alertly and purely at all times. . . . A person ought to know, not just when you're breaking with them, but when you're enthusiastic and less enthusiastic and a lot less enthusiastic. I mean, it's not just "Everything's fine until it's war." It's a dailiness. I believe it is part of our responsibility to each other. I guess my ideal is a kind of artistic creation and a kind of living, too, in which we enable each other to live by those little signals from now, now, now. . . . I think there are these innumerable little nuancy decisions you make . . . all those little revelations of where you are, you know, where your priorities are, and how they might better be. . . . There are a million little signals.[7]

There are, we know all too well, so many ways to miss each other, to even profit in our wicked way—temporarily at least—by making less-than-true impressions in our interactions with people, the easy money and the quick fix of purposefully false signals. It's a popular way of getting by and making a killing, of hurrying up and mattering. And then there's the clear note of nuance, the live risk of candor. Might we try to hold the world with a degree of affection and the openheartedness affection enables? What if all the world's a stage and it all turns on affection? Shall we ring true and front no longer?

A single intake of breath is sufficient to bring us to the admission that trying to ring true is a very messy undertaking. Life comes to us, it seems, already divided and, in more ways than we can keep track of, we already feel so devastatingly compromised. For this reason alone, the divisions feel so intensely helpful, almost salvific, a means for getting and staying ahead. I mean *really*, what *would* we do without them? But it is also the case that everything we have in the way of ancient wisdom in Scripture, story and song, whether in Shakespeare or Sanskrit, repeatedly tells us that these divisions are entirely untenable, destructive and—if it helps to put it this way—even heretical. We're called to pursue the slow and thoughtful work of resisting the haste of false witness despite the cost it might impose. True signals take time.

Courtesy of the heart might be the most countercultural—which is to say genuinely revolutionary—move we can make. It's also, in a sense that's obvious to anyone willing to slow down long enough to really think it through, the straightforward, ancient task of meeting the basic rule of neighborliness. To risk a hot-button word, courtesy of the heart is even a *conservative* hope, presuming we intend the word literally, because exercising our own powers of reference truly is, one would imagine, the first obligation of speech. ("This is that. And that has to do with this. And these two can't actually be rightly separated unless you're . . . you know . . . trying to sell something. Yourself, for instance.") In our words and our deeds and our deep-down imaginings of people and things, there are so many occasions—once more into the breach!—to try to be true, to begin to really see one another and thereby experience ourselves poetically.

EVERYTHING THAT EVER WAS AVAILABLE FOREVER

While I'd like to us to keep Wordsworth's nineteenth century jeremiad in mind lest we unduly conclude that we're in *completely* uncharted territory when it comes to the challenge of not losing our minds to technology completely, not being defeated by reality entirely and keeping before ourselves the possibility of neighborliness and goodwill, I'd nevertheless like us to consider courtesy of the heart in the light of and in spite of the flashing lights of all the electric soul molesters in our midst. Alongside Wordsworth's analysis, let's place novelist William Gibson's take on the state of everyday consciousness for many—most?—in what we're in the habit of conceiving as the developed world: "If you're fifteen or so, today, I suspect that you inhabit a sort of endless digital Now, a state of atemporality enabled by our increasingly efficient communal prosthetic memory. I also suspect that you don't know it, because, as anthropologists tell us, one cannot know one's own culture."[8]

What does courtesy of the heart—or even consistency of the heart—look like when the endless digital Now is always only one electronic appliance away, perhaps even signaling to you—and interrupting you—now within the space of time it takes to read this sentence? I don't have an answer, but I do have an anecdote. I was standing around talking to people at the conclusion of a house concert looking for reasons not to leave (they were incredibly interesting, my fellow attendees, and I couldn't help but want to meet all of them), and we got to talking about a song we wished the artist had included. "Which album is that on?" one of us asked. And the fellow we imagined might know stopped talking and stared into space.

Gesturing toward the device in the guy's front pocket, a friend broke the silence, "You know you could just . . ."

"No," he said, still staring. "I'm doing this the old way."

It was kind of a joke, except kind of not. And it spoke, as good jokes do, to the mess we're in. He really did access his memories old-school style, eventually recalling the album title and reveling in the fact that he could still do that kind of thing as if, one day, it'll be a kind of party trick. And let's remember—*re*member—that we can too. Our bodies are real. We can look people in the eye and listen and pay heed and recall things. We can actively treasure, value and take the time real presence requires. But it will probably involve a determined and deliberate embodiment. We'll often have to *decide* to do it. And we might find that an insistence on presence is something that many a neighbor (young and old) will often find off-putting, annoying and, given the taskmaster that phony motion is with its *Hurry up and matter!* alarm system, increasingly inappropriate and unprofessional. Perhaps that anxious future is already here, but it is of course difficult to know your own culture.

If we don't at least occasionally do it "the old way," the avenues for having a proper and functioning attention collection will likely disintegrate. What happens when almost everything appears to be one google away and yours for nothing save the willingness to sit still for it? Do hungry hearts still research the names in the liner notes, tracking down the source material of the things they love? Will there remain people in the world, human interest enough, willing to expend something like adequate attention on extraordinary offerings? The old way can begin to feel like the only way cultural treasures might go on *being treasured* by someone somewhere somehow whether it's reading a book all the way through or placing a needle on vinyl. The slow labor of discovery and the patience real amazement require is otherwise in danger of being lost.

This is the scenario writer-comedian Patton Oswalt believes places us "on the brink of Etewaf: Everything That Ever Was—Available Forever." As he describes our Etewaf moment, it's akin to the loss of topsoil and the accompanying disappearance of the conditions that make vegetation possible: "The topsoil has been scraped away, forever. . . . In fact, it's been dug up, thrown into the air, and allowed to rain down and coat everyone in a thin gray-brown mist called the Internet."[9] This is a powerfully apt image for articulating the challenge of somehow valuing and receiving—*really* receiving—the witness, the gift of insight, of any and every voice whose carefully rendered creative labor has come to be not just instantaneously ours for the taking, like water from a drinking fountain, but, God forbid, even tiresomely before us like dust we want to wipe off a table. If what once was treasured now feels disposable, how do we recover or conjure a context for receiving these gifts *as* gifts? Without the giving and receiving of vision—that's poetry by the way,

> **If what once was treasured now feels disposable, how do we recover or conjure a context for receiving these gifts *as* gifts?**

and gospel, too—the people will perish. It's as if there's hardly anyone left to actually pick up what's been laid down. And more broadly, how do we recover the gift of one another when there's always one more thing to be distracted but largely unmoved by? Can anyone anywhere get a witness anymore?

PEOPLE TAKE TIME

Gathering up what gifts of awareness remain and testifying to one another concerning their power is one of the primary responsibilities—and pleasures—of an aware people. And when it comes to the thinning out of consciousness that often seems to be occurring in the wake of our escalating distractedness, a profound commitment to courtesy of the heart in all things would appear to be our only hope. As it always has, the scope of my attention collection—my own personal canon, as it were—will be determined by who and what I'm willing and open to taking in, the questions and concerns I'll allow to matter to me. This is also where the dailiness of being true will play out in the sounding of a clear note or . . . won't so much. The Internet might intensify or quicken this process, making so much of it a part of the global public record in unprecedented ways, but the habits by which we deny ourselves to ourselves and others and those by which we come to consciousness remain perhaps essentially the same. It is indeed a new frontier when someone I haven't seen in over a decade suddenly appears—if it can be called an appearance—to wordlessly post a climate denial video on what was an otherwise calm and reasoned Facebook thread. But the challenge to try to imagine the person's context and the fact of their desire to somehow be engaged and to honor—to even revere, if I can—their attempt to be meaningfully social is as it's always been. There are after all so many who have seen the desire and revered the attempt in me. I will doubtless require their patience again.

People take time. But in our haste, we size them up or cut them down to what we take to be a more manageable size, labeling people instead of trying to hear, understand or welcome them. And we love our labels as ourselves even as they don't—and can't—do justice to the complexity of our own lived lives or anyone else's. It's as if we'll do anything to avoid the burden of having to think twice. To form an opinion about someone or something is to assert—or to believe we've asserted—some kind of control. And in the rush to opine, we degrade ourselves and whatever it is we'd like to think we've spoken meaningfully about and defensively stick to hastily prepared and unconvincing scripts, as others have before us, of radical denial. In this race to matter, to be in control and to somehow magically inspire our own confidence, it might be right to say, as I once heard my student Maggie Kinnucan observe, that we're all propagandists now.

People take time. And with a natural sense of awe that drops upon us as if by miracle every so often, we occasionally manage to look upon others with a deep sense of gladness. A recent formulation of this phenomenon comes to us from the character Theodore Twombly, played by Joaquin Phoenix in Spike Jonze's *Her*. Via the kind of earpiece and microphone one can witness in use in cars and on sidewalks whenever you see a person speaking personably into what appears to be thin air, Twombly's pouring his heart out to an operating system endowed with an artificial intelligence with whom he's falling in love. She's christened herself "Samantha," and Twombly's more relaxed and talkative than he's been in months. In the middle of a long night of people watching, he describes an experiment he likes to undertake: "Sometimes I look at people, and I make myself try and feel them as more than just a random person walking by."

I love his deployment of the word "sometimes." It's a startling and moving admission that his experience of other human beings as random and generally uninteresting isn't some kind of exception, but the norm. In his performance of the duties of recognition, of understanding that there's a unique somebody in each of the bodies passing by, he's only gone so far. But with delight, he notes that he'll sometimes risk the pleasure of trying to see—trying to actually feel—a stranger's presence as something more. It's an expenditure of effort for Twombly, but in the context of this exchange, he speaks as one convinced that it's very much worth it.

No One Has Meaning Alone

As the film proceeds, we're made to see that Twombly has a ways to go, but this statement is an early indicator that, like a once definitively disappointed child trying to try again, he's ready to recognize and to relish the quandary that is the living fact of other people. It's as if, despite himself, he feels compelled to widen his vision enough to allow another person to signify in some way, to mean something that surpasses or moves to the side of what he habitually takes them to be. How else can Twombly or any of us place ourselves in the path of beauty or reside in the way of the gift? It's a moment of surrender certainly, but this is the way it goes with feelings. And no one gets to have meaning alone.

This too is a courtesy of the heart, that trading of signals whereby we enable one another to live. "Nuancy decisions," Stafford calls them. No right relationship, it seems to me, without nuance. And no nuance until I allow others—ever so gingerly—to tell me what I appear to be up to. I'm not, as it turns out, the best or final authority concerning my own meaning. Everyone needs at least one or two people asking them—sometimes begging them—to tell them specifically how they're doing in this unfolding tale of trying to be true. They'll need certain assurances that I'm genuinely seeking their counsel, but people know when you're really asking. It's a commitment to a long and delicate conversation, and it can't be hurried. We get to put the request to folks every so often: "Tell me how I'm doing. Tell me the truth about where you think I am."

Life's too short to not do this. Life's too short to pretend that we already have when we haven't, or that we are when we honestly aren't. There are those who are in an especially good position to tell me the truth, because they're the unique recipients of my many assurances and signals, whether clear or purposefully unclear, true or false, my betrayals as well as my promises. I have to listen to these people. My life, if it's to be at all examined, requires their counsel, because we are, after all, connected. I am *in* relationship.

Religion is the what, the to whom, and the how of our everyday lives. And the ties, it shouldn't be controversial to observe, are a living fact, non-

> **Religion is the what, the to whom, and the how of our everyday lives.**

optional.[10] As I've argued, this word, carefully considered, names the fact of relationship rather well, but if it's just too radioactive, too fraught with tragedy and manipulation to be useful to some, it can be let go. I'm not trying to push a word.

But relation—now *there's* a word—can't be consistently denied without loss of life. Life's too short to pretend you're not in relationship or that you're not beholden to someone, many someones, in fact. How do we begin to overcome the widely broadcast distortions, without and within, that insist otherwise and degrade us so? How might we recover ourselves?

6

The web, the net and the verse

That feeling of a baby's brow against the palm
of your hand—how I have loved this life.

John Ames in Marilynn Robinson's *Gilead*

AS OF THIS WRITING, NATIONAL PUBLIC RADIO reports that membership in the Southern Baptist Convention is in decline for the seventh straight year, church attendance is decreasing steadily and baptisms are down. As I've made clear, I'm a *huge fan* of baptism, and membership—of the most human-thriving sort—is something I want for everyone. Church attendance? I don't actually think such a thing is possible, because I don't believe a person can attend (or even skip, exactly) the community of people one could rightly speak of as church. I'm such a stickler for these things—and yes, it could be either the neurosis or the wisdom at work—that I've trained my children to speak of the place to which we drive together at least once a week as church *building*.

We do attend the *meeting* of the church, we might say, in an effort to "forsake not the fellowship," as my grandmother might put it, quoting the Epistle to the Hebrews. But I want to get the words right. I want to keep us all in the way of the gift. I want them to think of church as a mobile assemblage of folks we know and are coming to know, dead and alive and still to come, who are uniquely committed to the living out of neighborliness and conviviality. And it's incredibly important to me that they not confuse these people and their living relationship to them with any institutional structure or [face in hands] building. Will Campbell, who worked alongside Martin Luther King Jr. and fought for desegregated schools and lunch counters in the civil rights era while also seeking relationship with incarcerated Klansmen, asserted that *church* is a verb, a peopled activity that, in one sense, ends when an institution (or a building) begins. I want them to think of being *in church* as being in the middle of a work of art, a collective witness of fellow human beings, wherever they are and whatever they're up to.

I share this vision of communal thriving and the difficulty of telling its stories with numbers as a way to begin expressing my sympathy and kinship with the individuals pollsters refer to as the "Nones,"[1] the supposedly "Religiously Unaffiliated" who make up roughly one-fifth of the American public (one-third of adults under thirty). I have a thing for the alleged Nones. I see a people uniquely interested in *not* unthinkingly drinking the proffered Kool-Aid and inspiringly aware of the dangers of doing so. Faced with the question of "present religion," one can be forgiven—or maybe even congratulated—for looking over some of the options (Protestant, Roman Catholic, Jewish, Muslim, Hindu, atheist) and initially seeing bigotry and boundaries. Aren't these divisions part of the problem? Why the one but not the other? Buddhist but in no way agnostic? Protestantism cut off from Catholicism *and* Judaism? Might there be lines of continuity among the multiple choice "answers"? Can we believe more than one thing? Can I see myself as something of a hybrid or perhaps write in an affiliation with the Jedi? Aren't we all made up of a wide variety of influences (like the proffered affiliations themselves)? Too easy an identification with one affiliation to the exclusion of the other can get to feeling like the same sad, dysfunctional song of too many a century. The labels we claim are conveniences, only ringing partially true—if at all—and never telling the whole story. If the Spirit blows wherever he wills, across and beyond whatever boundaries we presume into existence, why credit these divisions? It's more complicated than a casual circling can say. And an unexamined religion is not worth having.

The rise of the Nones—not that it's possible for a human being to be such a thing—is a positive turn that recognizes we are each the sum of many affiliations, more than anyone can possibly keep track of. As much as we love our labels as ourselves, the idea that anyone is ever only formed by a single religious tradition is a central fallacy of our time. Contrary to the suggestion that Millennials, for instance, are shallow characters unplugged from lives of meaning and generally just coasting, I spy people who long deeply for the real deal, who are committed to operating more critically concerning the suffering produced by being plugged in unthinkingly to any number of things and who appear determined to coast no longer. When I consider the foodies and food trucks, the artisan backlash that has so many of my former students diving into woodwork, pottery and all manner of sustainability (easy fodder—I know—for the *Portlandia* series, but a body has to start somewhere), I see people running *toward* a deeper awareness of relationship, not from it, people *more* alert and alive to the ways we have of depleting our own value, not less. *True religion.* Let us count the ways we long for it in song and dance and getting and spending. Those who don costumes and formal party attire to register enthusiasm at an Arcade Fire concert or decide to have song lyrics, a phrase from Shakespeare or a Wendell Berry quotation tattooed on an arm have not, to my mind, lost the plot; they're looking to become more meaningfully invested and knowingly situated *in* it, in spite of its daily elusiveness. They're looking to expand—not close—their circles of sympathy. What else is a lifetime for? More and more are wonderfully willing to risk getting caught believing in something. My inner-Dostoevsky adds that a good many also like to be *seen* believing it and post the pictures to prove it.

You Have a Body. Just Admit It.

I'm heartened by these phenomena because they strike me as instances of people deciding to own their own enthusiasms in a more embodied way. They are one step in the lifework of seeing what we're scared of, deeply acknowledging what we're hoping for and no longer living in defensive denial of our own raw vulnerability. The absolute importance of leveling with ourselves concerning our sacred desire to be a part *of* something (so easily exploited and perversely applied) instead of standing apart *from* everything and everyone (as strong and in control as that makes us feel) is at the heart of my plea that we stop pretending we aren't religious. To disavow religiousness by insisting that we're *spiritual* but not religious is an understandable move given the violent rage the Western world is prone to assign to the catch-all abstraction "religion." But because we are mutually caught up in the life of the rest of the world in all that we say, do and consume, the disavowal doesn't stand up to scrutiny. To decree, "I'm spiritual but not religious," as Phyllis Tickle reminds us, is a little like saying, "I'm human but not flesh and bone." I too have a body, a body that needs things, does things and pursues them in particular ways. It is by way of my own particular religiosity that I participate and am, in fact, implicated in the lives of others. To think I'm capable of opting out—or to honestly believe I've done so with a bored shrug—is to think like a sociopath. It's disconcerting to try to have a conversation with people who speak as if they don't possess a particular point of view, but this habit is legion among us. It isn't only other people, we must admit, who live within a context.

When we really admit to the fact of our own context, we're less prone to deny others the complications of their own and empathy becomes a living possibility. In this sense, the good news about weird religious backgrounds is that we all have one, and there are as many as there are people. Numbering ourselves *among* those who conduct their lives according to strange ideas about the world, acting out one form of devotion after another, whether inspired or ill-conceived, means refusing to keep ourselves aloof from the rest of humanity and accepting a place among our fellow pilgrims also searching for meaning, also trying to make sense of their own lives, and also living with the difficult and pressing question of what to do in light of what we know. We begin to take up the task of empathy when we're susceptible to the sense that the inner lives of others might be as real and as realistic as our own.

> **The good news about weird religious backgrounds is that we all have one.**

I would suggest that we can't even begin to do so until we stop denying the living fact of our own religiosity. And in our day, I believe the denial has taken on the power of a pathology, a trick we play on ourselves which makes it possible to reduce another person or an entire region of the world utterly. We cut the complexity of their existence down to manageable size with the application of the word "religious," so that infinitely valuable human beings are shut up and squared away, successfully oversimplified in our minds forever. It's such a mean, limiting, dishonest move, a simple and convenient way of closing the doors on most of the world, keeping certain ethical headaches at bay and relieving ourselves of the burden of thinking about them. As the poet Geoffrey Hill reminds us, "Tyranny requires simplification."[2]

I propose that we begin to swear off this habitual gesture of disavowal, this alarmingly uncool move. It can feel like a risky surrender to the chaos of other people, near and far, the family member *and* the beleaguered foreigner, whose lives we'd like to keep outside the borders of our own, to let religion name what *we're* up to as well as what *they* are in all they do, think and dream (since we've likely already fooled ourselves into thinking in the easy and deadly binary of Us and Them). Yet it returns us to the crucial recognition of our common human condition, a vision of neighborliness within which we might begin to credit others with something approaching the intelligence with which we long to be credited.

We are of course welcome to find one another's fervently held ideas about life and how to live it, the world, and God or no god perfectly ridiculous, but we need to remain *in* a conversation to have one. "Well, I'm not religious, so . . ." gets played like a trump card. If the word applies to thee but never to me, I've made a distinction that is an ultimately isolating move. I stand on the higher ground of reasoned detachment while you're inevitably awash in folklore and craziness yet again. Am I permitted to feel isolated and disconnected from your strange convictions? Absolutely. But I'm putting on a front (frontin', as the parlance of hip-hop has it) if I presume there's nothing strange about my own, that I see clearly where others only see confusedly. I'm forsaking the possibility of fellowship, of seeing myself as one avid pilgrim among others, as I resort to the intellectual laziness of snobbery, that refuge of the shallow. It's a dead end. As MC Breed admonishes us, there's no future in your frontin'.

ALL IMAGINATION, ALL THE TIME

The *feeling* of disconnectedness from what someone else believes is a fact that gives us something interesting and even wonderful to talk about. But to claim or insinuate disconnection *as* a fact, as if we've extracted ourselves from the social world, the labor and patience of others upon whom our livelihoods depend, is to live in delusion and denial. The more difficult and excellent way is to live without alibis and without succumbing to the tired temptation to front with one another, to concretely own up to also being situated so that I see my life as morally answerable to the people around me. I don't believe I can even begin to do this as long as I honestly think I can sidestep the question of religion, because it is precisely nothing less than the question of my own devotion. Needless to say, *religious* devotion, like a religious value, a religious priority or a religious ritual, is, to my mind, a hopeless redundancy. Think about it.

Religion, after all, is nothing if not relationship, the way I go about relating to the world made plainly evident by the forms my relating takes. And relationship, like culture, is nonoptional. I'm always cultivating and relating in one way or another, whether generously or mercilessly, whether with care and caution or in a pinched, fearful, endlessly defensive fashion. Like any relationship, religion can be very bad, but it can also be very good. It can be true, and it can be devastatingly false, this way we have of dealing, coping and managing ourselves and others. In this sense, the question of religion is always the question of right relationship, a question that can't be justly avoided by anyone anywhere. It's a question that comes to us in our dreams when we try to.

And if I might be permitted a reference to a figure within the dark depths of the Marvel Universe, right religion will always depend on what we do or fail to do with what Steve Ditko's Doctor Stephen Strange once referred to as "the basic power of the imagination." Everything turns upon it, swaying us to the mood of what we like or loathe. An early Strange tale featured the good Doctor performing acts of saving wizardry on behalf of the inhabitants of a village in the Bavarian Alps who have been possessed by hostile spirits from another dimension. In his final standoff with an incorporeal being that had overcome the mind of the village's hapless mayor, Strange responds to the poltergeist's final taunt with an overpowering spell: "There is no power greater than that which I possess for mine is the basic power of the imagination, the gossamer threads of which dreams are woven."[3]

What we weave and, more disturbingly, what we find woven around us in binding images, ideas and stories about the way the world works is ultimately decisive in the way we conduct ourselves, what we fear, bet on and hope for in all we do. When our imagination is transformed, culture follows, and when it has hardened past the point of yielding to insight, we the people perish. Whether it's a trap or a means of transport, the tangled web of what we're able to imagine, the meanings we assign and design in the spaces we're in, defines our lives. And our capacity for illusion is limitless.

As counterintuitive as it might seem, the essential ethical task of being a part of where I live, of being a body meaningfully present among and to my family and surrounding community, is one with the work of imagination. Right livelihood begins with right conception, and because I can't easily conceive the web of relationships out of which, say, an affordable cup of coffee is placed before me, I am compelled to try to imagine it as justly and realistically as I can. To *see* truly in spite of all that I can't *know*, I have to try to *imagine*. No neighborliness, we might say, without a careful and far-reaching imagination—reaching beyond, for instance, the question of how inexpensive the coffee is for me and toward the lengthy liturgy involving those who grew, cultivated and picked the beans and hopefully own the land on which they labored. So much depends on where we go with our imaginations.

Inescapable Network of Mutuality

There is *so much* that serves to obscure the fact of where I am and the fact of what my own doing does; so much in the way of shame, oversimplification, messaging, slogan, advertising and other people's talking points can prevent me from interpreting my own experience well. If I only imagine in broad strokes and generalizations (you can pick them out freely from the nearest headlines: criminals, fundamentalists, immigrants, racists, terrorists, the rich, the unemployed), the living fact of the world I'm in and the neighborly role available to me within it can elude me indefinitely. When I'm overwhelmed by the dominant and dominating version—or perversion—of reality that would cut us all down to the size of caricature and "use-value," I'm blinded to all manner of redemptive possibility in my daily existence and largely robbed of the beautifully complex presence of others as they are of mine.

An admonition against this everyday failure of imagination comes to us in Flannery O'Connor's famously subversive assertion: "Somewhere is better than anywhere."[4] I take it to be a provocatively countercultural and commonsensical call to not be in perpetual flight, to not be always elsewhere in mind and spirit, reaching after the false promise of one more immortality project. It's a call to make instead that rare saving choice to be alive to where you are situated, to be more radically present—I'm tempted to say religiously present—to where you are and to whom you'd do well to feel grateful, obliged and related. O'Connor calls me to touch what's beneath, around or nearby me to better orient myself, to make the whole world kin.

Like the alternative habit of being that O'Connor's wise saying invites us to take on, the crisis she addresses isn't *uniquely* religious but *universally* so, because everyone is situated, alive and interpreting; everyone is in, among and in interaction with the visions and artifacts of others. That we're tied up with one another is a fact. How we address the fact is the perpetual question of what we do with our own self-understanding, our own voices, our own vocations. Thinking of the question *as* religious helps me to scrutinize those parts of my life that would otherwise too easily escape my attention.

I have in mind here Martin Luther King Jr.'s phrase in the Birmingham epistle, words which invite us to see ourselves more realistically and responsibly by recognizing that our lives are caught up and sustained within an "inescapable network of mutuality." No unrelated people. No isolated facts. Everything we do or neglect to do, in this religious sense, counts when we allow ourselves to be "cognizant of the interrelatedness of all communities and states."[5] King's vision isn't simply a beautiful picture but rather a summons to moral seriousness, a breakthrough if we'll let it be, and a challenge to see ourselves as members of one another and, by doing so, to *re*member well in the way we esteem our fellow human beings near and far. The deep realism to which he invites us to orient our thinking and doing is the deep relatedness against which national boundaries, ethnic divisions and class structures appear as the consensual fictions they ultimately are. Do we have the eyes and wit to perceive as much? Do we want to?

To see truly is to see seriously. The Buddhist monk Thich Nhat Hanh offers a quick beginner's course in doing so in his consideration of the source material and the human resourcefulness hidden within a single sheet of paper. Holding one up, he asks us what we see. Paper? Yes, but what else? Hanh invites us to look harder by imagining more: "If you are a poet, you will see clearly that there is a cloud floating in this sheet of paper."

How can this be? It's an awareness of process. We see that a cloud has to be there as we recall the fact that a tree requires rain. There's also the sun. There's a lumberjack present too *and* what the lumberjack had for breakfast that tree-felling morning *and* the farms on which the items in that breakfast were produced. We also might notice the lumberjack's father and mother. To begin to imagine these connections—and again, they don't require our imagining or our awareness to be living facts—through the living fact of interrelation is to begin to imagine with sacred nuance. Far from being an escape into disembodied bliss or fancy, this sensibility dissolves whatever dichotomies might keep us from perceiving and responding to the complex relatedness of all of life. It is a call to a deeper investment in the given world than our usual ways of construing the world allow. And lest we miss the call by referring to Hanh's teaching as a *spiritual* perspective concerning a piece of paper, please note that Hanh, King, O'Connor and their ilk are inviting us to think more realistically, not less. Answering the call to consciousness begins with the determination to be realistic by being awake to the everyday liturgies we personally undertake as well as those of others, the liturgies of other people upon whom our own lives depend.

If I'm to be a person of *good* faith, each day is an occasion to imagine with greater accuracy and appreciation the net, the latticework, in which I'm caught up, the labor out of which my life has been made possible, and to experience the fact of my relatedness as a gift and a responsibility. To conduct my life in *bad* faith is to proceed in denial of this relatedness in speech, action and investment. The avenues for proceeding in bad faith are myriad and multiplying, often appearing before us as the only means for, as the saying goes, *getting ahead.*

What I do with a strange phrase like "getting ahead" will depend on how I go about imagining my own context. What's forward and what's backward? Who do I hope to get ahead of, and where do I imagine I'm getting *to*, exactly? Does it include playing well with others? Do I resent even being made to ask these questions?

PEOPLE WILL DO ANYTHING TO ALLEVIATE THEIR ANXIETY

One of the thrills of watching the conniving, the betrayals, the bad judgments and the genuine moments of genius and grace among the characters of the *Mad Men* series is the way we're treated to the dramatizing of one neurosis after another. In a profound sense, their struggles are ours. Advertising may play necessarily on our dreams and our rutting discontent, but it only hits its target because the likes of Don Draper and Peggy Olson have learned to get their own hearts written out on legal pads and conjured into images with the help of attentive illustrators. The most intense epiphanies seem to occur when Don, our lead visionary for hire, gets lost in thoughtful reverie and speaks aloud, from beyond analysis or control, like the forsaken and curious child he forever remains.

"What is it like to have someone's life in your hands?" he asks his heart surgeon neighbor Arnold Rosen in a rare instance of voiced-aloud wonder before seeing him off on skis in a blizzard through New York streets to perform life-saving surgery. It's a significant moment in the series because, whether we recall his three children, his wives, his coworkers, his brother, his lovers or the millions who buy the products whose near-perfect pitches he's cobbled together with (or stolen from) others, we can easily put together the fact that there's hardly a life within the scope of the show that *hasn't* passed through his hands. As much as he might like to think otherwise, Don Draper, like the rest of us, is never *not* mattering. Will he ever allow himself a consistently genuine waking life? Can an ad man afford such a thing?

Arnold surprises him by saying, as if it's obvious, that decisions in which *lives are at stake* are a part of the privilege and responsibility with which "guys like us" are entrusted. "Guys like us?" Don asks with a puzzled look.

Arnold lays it out. They're both in the people business, responding to, capitalizing on or anticipating the whole gamut of human anxiety: "You get paid to think about things they don't like to think about, and I get paid to *not* think about them." And then, more enigmatically: "People will do anything to alleviate their anxiety."

And . . . cut to another scene featuring Don in bed again with another lonely soul, consensually kidding himself together with a fellow person of faith, another hungry heart, his anxiety getting the best of him in all-too-costly fashion one more time. We find him where we loved him and left him, a weary knight of uncommendable faith not, as it turns out, hurtling toward self-discovery and the way of the gift just yet.

Those who love him the most are often the most eloquent witnesses to Don's standard operating procedures. Letting him have it in a train station, his teenage daughter, Sally, notes what happens whenever anyone pays him any attention, "and they *always* do . . . you just *ooze* everywhere." What to do with the drive to ooze? *Mad Men* raises questions to which it offers no definitive answers, and the big one that asks what scenarios or insights might finally render Don Draper bona fide remains as elusive for the series as it does for the rest of us. How do we alleviate our anxiety non-destructively?

I know no quick fixes, but I do have an attention collection. Even if my teaching gig didn't afford me the joy of trying to relate one thing to another for a living, the treasuring of the jarring image, passage, lyric or verse would still serve, as it always has, to get me unstuck, a little more vigilant against Draper-typical fantasy enactment, and that extra bit alive to nearby joys from which I'm otherwise too easily distracted. In what I hope might be called something approaching good faith, I seek that finer tale of who we are and what we're up to, those creative offerings—it could be a moment in a pop song—which seem to place reality, even if only for a few fleeting seconds, in a truer perspective, reviving and directing me toward the fact of where I am.

I have available to me, for instance, Marilynne Robinson's John Ames of *Gilead*, who knows something about our inescapable network of mutuality—think *way of the gift*—and the joys and the duties of right reverence when holding someone's life in your hands. He describes holding an infant as follows:

> While I was holding her, she opened her eyes. I know she
> didn't really study my face. Memory can make a thing seem
> to have been much more than it was. But I know she did look
> right into my eyes. That is something. . . . I realize there is
> nothing more astonishing than a human face. . . . You feel your
> obligation to a child when you have seen it and held it. Any
> human face is a claim on you, because you can't help but un-
> derstand the singularity of it, the courage and loneliness of it.
> But this is truest of the face of an infant. I consider that to be
> one kind of vision, as mystical as any.[6]

In *every face* a claim. There is so much here to stop us in our tracks,
to summon us to reverence, to prompt us to ask what in hell we
think we mean when we tell ourselves we're on the verge of getting
ahead. Ames knows that the mind plays tricks, but he is compelled
to brood on the stewardship of astonishment, of learning and responding to the beauty at work in any human face. One can spy an
entire doctrine of the sacred here in this short passage on living,
seeing and knowing artfully in which Ames seamlessly unites
ethics with aesthetics and compassion. How could we forget that
they're one? I think of one especially nervy moment with Don
Draper exclaiming, "I don't have time for art!" as he rushes off to
get his foot in the door of another fantasy. It's what we do. We can't
be made to see.

Preemptive Sympathy

The courage and loneliness of another person's face draws on me
and claims me, because *I cannot help but understand* their singular
relation to my own. I'm called to see myself within their vision, to
begin to see myself as they might see me, and the resulting vision
is indeed mystical, because so much remains concealed in the fact
of communion, that space in which we experience ourselves as

undeniably related, as kindred, knowing it all a joy. To be in communion with others is to recognize that I can't be myself to myself without imagining them well and therefore justly. Again, the question of art, the question of how and what I imagine is everything.

As I understand him, Ames is describing what the mad farmer-poet Wendell Berry refers to as "preemptive sympathy," that task of attentiveness by which we begin to "recognize with sympathy the fellow members, human and nonhuman, with whom we share our place." It isn't a once-for-all achievement so much as a habit we find ourselves taking up or tragically putting aside many times a day. Some form of preemptive sympathy is, I suspect, a prerequisite of good faith which, for Berry, achieves visible, words-made-flesh form in the occurrence of affection: "As imagination enables sympathy, sympathy enables affection. And it is in affection that we find the possibility of a neighborly, kind, and conserving economy."[7]

I love it when Wendell Berry speaks of conserving things, because the mere thought of him reminds me of all the ways a radioactive word like "conservative" might still be properly sounded with a sense of due heft. There's a degree of sneakiness involved, but I enjoy telling my students that I'd never risk the presumption and hubris of calling myself conservative, because such an assessment could only *maybe* be appropriate at the conclusion of my life, made by people in a position to make that call. What did I manage to conserve and share for the good of whose commonwealth? Was my life a tale of neighborliness or largely one of fear and defensiveness? What did I really do with what affection I had?

These questions are sobering, but they enliven me even as they center me, even as they make me feel the poverty of so much of what I do and say when I ignore them. The good news is that, at any moment, I can change the story I'm telling myself. And in its appeal to my imagination, God's kingdom comes little by little, one recognition at a time. With an eye on *oikos* as Greek for "household" and

at the root of the term "economy" (recall the psalmist famously
hoping that he might dwell, as the Septuagint renders it, in the *oikos*
of God forever), Wendell Berry suggests that we might free this
sacred vision of its sectarian associations, as well as our own tendency to assume we already know all about it, by referring to the
kingdom of God as the Great Economy. It's that sacred vision of a
membership that excludes nothing and no one and within which
everything we do or don't
do signifies.[8] Such sacred visions beckon me to turn my
imagination back toward the
human circle, to locate my

> **The good news is that, at any
> moment, I can change the
> story I'm telling myself.**

existence within it and to ask myself how far I'll allow my sympathy
to reach, to *re*member despite the fact of a culture that often appears hell-bent on *dis*membering our understanding of ourselves
at every turn. What might it mean to seek first the Great Economy
and the right relations it engenders?

True Religion

Hungering and thirsting for righteousness begins by really imagining myself as a stakeholder in the lives of others, by seeing myself
somehow—not merely figuratively—holding their lives in my hands
as they hold mine in theirs. If my religion is my relationship to the
world, good religion would be the work of developing, growing and
deepening consciousness, not closed, shut, settled, rigid or done for,
but one of ever-unfolding receptivity and, if you like, continual repentance, a continual turning away from all of my not-quite-
worthy-of-life commitments, a way of taking responsibility for
what I do. In this sense, it seems to me that owning this relationship
as religion is a requirement of good faith and therefore a step in the
direction of true religion. Bad faith begins in the disavowal that will
own up to little or nothing. And in turn, bad religion is the dis-

avowal of relationship, a denial made plain in any practice we have for dividing ourselves from others, those ways we have of turning away from the fact of kinship.

I would argue that one such practice, peculiarly predominant and damaging in the activities of our westernizing world, is the rhetorical strategy that only conceives religion as someone else's problem, as if we've magically removed ourselves from the complexities of relationship. When we're enmeshed in bad religion, we have a way of denying the fact of our own bodies and degrading and destroying the bodies of others. Oversimplification kills. It always has.

Good religion cherishes bodies, and it is evident in any practice that restores, reinforces, reconsiders and redeems the human form, locating it, in Thoreau's phrase, as "a part and parcel of nature."[9] Good religion is at work in the cultivation of consciousness and in all that involves us in seeing ourselves truly, in experiencing ourselves—and helping others experience themselves—anew. We know it when we see it, and we learn it, necessarily, by heart.

We risk falling into deluding abstraction if we take the matter further and speak too knowingly or boastfully of *true* religion. But lest we grow too abstract in our thinking about such a thing, a very helpful text attributed to James, the brother of Jesus of Nazareth, maintains that one sure sign of true religion would be the lived concern for orphans and dispossessed women.[10] When we think of it this way, we're invited to view at least one indication of true religion as plainly discernible among pockets of people the world over, people united in spite of a wide variety of confessions (including atheism). I say we refrain from calling them "Nones."

Admittedly, this straightforwardly humble standard for crediting one another as sound can frustrate those of us—our number is legion—who tend to place the litmus test for faithfulness in the realm of what we say we believe about God or life after death or who should be accorded the legal right to marriage, but the modestly on-the-ground work of being good to people often proves to be a scandal to our egos. And the criteria for actual neighborliness, especially toward the vulnerable, remains eye-rubbingly clear most of the time. The demands of true love are almost scandalously obvious and much more demanding than saying or trying to convince others we believe certain impossible-to-prove things. Which is why, as Vincent Harding tells us, love trumps doctrine every time.[11]

The love that is true and therefore rightly trumps the age-old fuss over who believes what—that love against which there is no legitimate law—is much more commonplace than we're prone to recognize if we're regularly informed by the hysterical talking points of those who profit (or believe they profit) from stoking the fires of fear and resentment in our vision of those who appear bitterly foreign to us in a zero-sum game of a world. There are better ways of viewing those souls whose names we find it difficult to spell and pronounce, human faces by whom we won't be moved or astonished so long as we're willingly enlisted into narratives of bitterness and diminishment when it comes to our fellow humans. Though they might not get any screen time, one can see every day that there are blessed people, here, there and everywhere, hungering and thirsting for righteousness, committed to taking care of the otherwise disinherited among us (which, apart from certain infrastructures available to some but not to all, is *any* one of us at so many points in our lives) and longing for a future in which everyone has what they need to thrive. There are solid people everywhere, it turns out. True religion springs eternal every once in a while.

It springs whenever we're awakened by a vision of ourselves as wonderfully and undeniably bound to others within the beauty, the darkness and the complexity of what I find it very helpful to refer to as the Verse, that sanity-restoring colloquialism for the visible universe I borrow from the interplanetary culture of Joss Whedon's

Firefly series. Removing the uni (*unus* is Latin for "one"), Whedon's far-flung space pilgrims in the future see the totality of existence (*versum*—a rotation, a row, a turning) as a process of change. What a way of putting it. When we speak of the Verse, we draw on a humble but imaginative posture that envisions what we feel we know of reality—the felt truth of a "known universe" we have to see feelingly to see at all—as a kind of row that human consciousness hoes as well as it can in its discerning of worlds in flux. Like "As far as I know" or "I can only imagine," it asserts the fallibility of the speaker who might otherwise be understood as speaking too knowingly.

In *Firefly*, the human population knows the dangers of speaking too knowingly. Though humanity persists, the earth itself has been lost apart from a lingering imagery of ecological loss due to war and other misconceptions of profit and a few surviving artifacts from Earth-That-Was. The Verse, then, comes to us as a hard-won expression with its own history of love and loss. What we think we know of the place we're in, as the characters on *Firefly* read the situation, is best understood as a deep furrow or an emplotment which, like the framing of poetic verse, is the asserting of a space of witness, a vision yielding the scope of something taken in, something experienced and also unfolding, environing before our eyes and beyond our ability to account for it. When I think of the Verse, I recall that I myself am sustained by others' feats of attentiveness, their know-how, candor, honest intuition, and their hungering and thirsting for righteousness. I receive from them, as I like to think others will in turn receive from me in a bundle of belonging that isn't just a sense or a feeling but a cosmic fact.

A Person Is a Person Through Other Persons

"That feeling of a baby's brow against the palm of your hand—how I have loved this life." We return to John Ames in an unintended almost haiku of a sigh. And it testifies further to the cosmic fact—or the feeling of the cosmic fact—many of us are learning to associate with the possibility of living, seeing and thinking wisely, of situating ourselves rightly in relation to others. It's the concept of Ubuntu, a gift of human discernment coming from the Nguni people of southern Africa and popularized by Desmond Tutu, who describes it as both "the very essence of being human" *and* that core quality of human kindness our interactions will bear witness to, or, to our detriment, disavow. Because awakening and embodiment go together, Ubuntu is the knowledge out of which arises the practices of generosity, hospitality and compassion which *say*—as only actions can—that "my humanity is caught up, is inextricably bound up, in yours." We see most feelingly that "We belong in a bundle of life" and that "A person is a person through other persons." In welcome tension with the estranging emphasis on individual identity we associate with Cartesian dualism ("I think, therefore I am"), Ubuntu asserts, "I am human because I belong. I participate, I share." To have a sense of Ubuntu restored is to experience oneself connected again. Tutu lays it out:

> A person with *Ubuntu* is open and available to others, affirming of others, does not feel threatened that others are able and good, he or she has a proper self-assurance that comes from knowing that he or she belongs in a greater whole and is diminished when others are humiliated or diminished, when others are tortured or oppressed, or treated as if they were less than they are. . . . To forgive [in this sense] is not just to be altruistic. It is the best form of self-interest.[12]

That feeling of known belonging is the literacy, so easily lost, of how to be—and know oneself to be—together with people. And it is a literacy we never stop learning, a literacy of wonder. In my efforts to lift up the ancient vision of Ubuntu as a standard in my own mind and to commend it to others, characterizing it as a *religious* vision would serve no helpful end at all. For one thing, I don't think it's possible for a vision to *not* be religious, and for another, decreeing it religious only makes it easier for many a contemporary mind to reject it with all the weird and bitterly anxious divisions of self from others such a rejection makes inevitable.

But the question of religion, the way we relate to the world, falsely, truly, badly or healthily, remains before us. And I believe it is most profoundly addressed when we see it as indistinguishable from the question of membership. Of what whole do I perceive or know myself to be a member when I place my hand on the brow of a baby or a child or even a full-grown human? If I feel myself awash in love of the life I share with the sometimes courageous and sometimes lonely face of my fellow member with whom I've exchanged this intimacy, will I proceed accordingly? Will I live up to the claims of my intense recognitions, or will I detach myself in the hope of achieving something more secure? Does my mind trail off to dream of somehow *maximizing* my position, of being more—what's that woefully unexamined word—impactful?

There are so many ways to lose a righteous sense of ourselves amid the demands and the perceived have-tos of our unbalanced and misperceiving world. But I can discover and reclaim my own membership anew at any time by way of the dignity and creativity I see and feel with others. I can bring what gifts I have to the flow of a gift economy upon which we've all along depended one more time, holding out my attention collection with open hands in expectation of receiving, once again, an education. I can recover the plot by leveling with myself concerning what I'm up to in my expenditure of energy and what it is I mean to do with my one wild and precious life.

And again, it's a work that's never exactly done, but it's also as straightforward as artfully recovering a kind of self-presence. Søren Kierkegaard describes it as a process we get to take up repeatedly if we're to receive a sense of our own context: "I should suppose that education was the curriculum one had to run through in order to catch up with oneself."[13] The curriculum comes to us through the attentive care of others, whether in lyric, image, conversation, remembrance or even a well-timed, open-ended question, and it is indeed geared toward a literacy of loving well. As Tutu tells us, this is the love that is actually self-interest at its poetic best. As that commonsensical paradox characteristic of the Ubuntu insight has it, it is only by really loving and forgiving others *as members of ourselves* that we can begin to really love, forgive or cherish ourselves at all.

The chother

In the prophets, we note that "the world"
is never generic; it is one's own world.

Daniel Berrigan,
Jeremiah: The World, the Wound of God

AND AGAIN WITH THE ATTENTION COLLECTION, I have a concept, sacred in my estimation, that arose from repeatedly leaving a child alone in front of a television. It's a serendipitous slip of the tongue I gleaned and now treasure from the testimony of my once-four-year-old son when he offered a commentary upon an iconic image within the Hanna-Barbera tradition. Giving voice to his specific love for the antics and escapades of Scooby-Doo and the community with whom he makes his way through a harried world, he once told me that he especially likes the moments in which Scooby and Shaggy get scared to the point of paralysis. In what I suspect is a touchstone in every episode, though I can't claim to have studied the matter thoroughly, there comes a time when Scooby and Shaggy respond to duress (a man in a monster costume, for instance) by leaping into one another's arms and quivering together for a couple of seconds, a precious moment in which it's hard to say where the dog stops and the man begins.

They hold *each other*, we might say, but in his effort to articulate what delighted him so, the child put it much, much better: "They hold their 'chother."

With the enunciation of this concept, that of *the chother*, I believe we're sitting squarely within the glow of a religious insight, an insight that meets all manner of resistance—*also* religious—in our hurry-up-and-matter, mad, mad world. First, the resistance. As I understand it, the idea that any of us can have our meaning alone or be the sole authors of our own significance or have joy for which we only have ourselves to thank is a death-dealing delusion. This psycho covenant implies, for instance, that a strong, successful few might somehow gain their lives without losing them, that there are those who have *earned*, *thought* or perhaps *bought* their way beyond the neediness—the essential vulnerabilities—of relationship. And as the delusion has it, there are those among us who through will, drive and ingenuity might somehow join them. Influencers? VIPs? High-impact people? Perhaps you know the parlance, or rather, the creeds.

The Movement of Anti-Grace

This bizarre and ineluctably religious vision of humanity is such an unacknowledged given in the popular thinking of the Western world, viewed so simply as *the way things work*, that it can feel awfully difficult to hold it at an angle or at arm's length long enough to consider the possibility that it might not be so. Pull yourself up by your own bootstraps, the saying goes, as if such a thing were possible. *Hard work pays off.* Well, of course. Yes. It *sometimes* does. Does this mean that anyone who isn't getting paid is probably in that pickle for lack of trying or that those who do get paid—and then some—have what they have for having labored so truly and excellently? *That* . . . would be an insane claim. And yet it's *so* in circulation, a myth perpetuated among adults like a handshake, a tale told to children as if it were gospel, a contagion we know to be very much airborne. When you begin to see it, you find that it's the default moral of . . . a very significant chunk of the best-selling contemporary tales of our time. Look at the books on display at the airport. Is it not the case that a sizable sum of the stories on offer give a moving account—you can skip to the end—of how someone hurried up and at long last mattered? Why are those faces on those magazines? These are the amazing people who finally got it together and really went for it. [eyes closed] All hail the power of the lone individual.

There are so many ways of naming this popular delusion. It's the very hubris that gets classically played out in song and story and on screen and stage repeatedly, and it's probably remembered and then quickly forgotten as a problem we ourselves might have numerous times on any given day. One very helpful naming of the evil spirit comes to us from the mind of writer George Monbiot, who gives to this otherwise airy nothing a local habitation and a name by describing and skewering the phenomenon as—wait for it—*the self-attribution fallacy.* Perhaps you've witnessed it: "This means crediting yourself with outcomes for which you weren't responsible." Ever discerned that little mind dance in action?

Think of self-attribution as the movement of anti-grace. It's the opposite of the way of the gift. This isn't to say that we bear no responsibility for any positive outcome. It's just that the conditions for thriving so many of us enjoy aren't *necessarily* the natural result of the reign of righteousness in the world. It wasn't all justice, we might say. An awful lot of what we have—clothes, computers, food, the abode in which we lay our heads to rest—arrive via "the ruthless exploitation of others and accidents of birth." Or in some cases, to put it more simply: "luck and brutality." We're fond of recalling aloud that we don't deserve what we have, but does that cliché go especially deep in our self-understanding? Does it play out in the way we like to see the lives of others ordered? Maybe not so much. Because this is all a "myth of election" so easily reduced to comedy the moment a sober person comes close to voicing it aloud, it can only thrive—and it really does—through insinuation and the explaining away of the lived tragedies of so many whose access to abundant life is blocked by the wicked ordering of life and resources we anxiously lobby to keep in place. Monbiot brings the whole house of cards down with a devastating analogy: "If wealth was the inevitable result of hard work and enterprise, every woman in Africa would be a millionaire."[1] Self-respect? Certainly. Love your neighbor as you love yourself? Of course. Come on, world, let's get started. Self-attribution? If that one has hold of you, you may as well be demon possessed. In fact, you kind of already are. Watch what happens when the teleprompter breaks.

In the Beginning Was Relationship

Scooby and Shaggy, meanwhile, hold their chother. Take a moment to think about it. The wondrous image is of course just one more iteration of the ancient, soul-savingly obvious but *still countercultural* realization that to be whole is to be part. If we hold to the chother principle, we understand again what we're hell-bent on denying and forgetting, that our very sustenance and whatever identity we can be said to have comes to us via the fact of relatedness or not at all. Just look at that social pipeline. It's Ubuntu all over again, because we can see that there's a kindness, a sweetness, that immediately follows the insight—that *is* the insight—that my own life can't be ultimately divided from the life of others or even defined at all except *by way* of others, *our chother*. I am because *we are*. Or as the Jewish mystic Martin Buber liked to say, in the beginning was relationship. Whether via the biblical injunction to die in order to live or the Buddhist principle of *anatta* (no-self), all manner of ancient wisdom counsels that whatever self I can be said to have is the gift of self I receive from my relation to others, the groundless ground (think of the way Shag and Scoob almost levitate) of the chother.

The realization of the social fact of the chother of course happens all the time. The hope that it might happen today, some lived experience of real community, is often what gets us out of bed in the morning. And of course, in what can be a slightly sad way, it's why we retreat to another screen. It's why we eavesdrop, and it's why we like to sit in bars and coffee shops. It's the way we look to a song. We ache for it. When we're confronted with crisis, when we join together in music or when we experience (or receive) a vision of soul, whatever the source, the question of where my one life starts and that of my neighbor stops begins to dissolve, and the bad, sad-making religion of hyperindividualism takes on an unreal and unseemly quality. By way of our chother, we begin to discern our true position in a fuller picture of the world we're in. We were never really able to take it all in by our lonesome anyway. It takes two to see.

In such moments, we're summoned not so much to act *as if* the road to life, loveliness, salvation and sane seeing can only be entered into where two or more are gathered, but rather to proceed in recognition of this sweet, scandalous, sometimes embarrassing fact. For one mad moment, we're relieved of the sociopathic burden of trying to convince ourselves and others we're self-made people who might matter just a little bit more than the average human. We get to give that heavy defensiveness up (deep down, we desperately hoped to, anyway). We get to find, hold on *and* let go within the circle of each other—our chother.

> **For one mad moment, we're relieved of the sociopathic burden of trying to convince ourselves and others we're self-made people who might matter just a little bit more than the average human.**

Life's too short to be lived in a swirl of perceived self-attribution, or rather, life can't begin to be properly perceived at all when we're in its throes, anxiously resistant to the grace that is the fact of the matter. God opposes the proud but gives grace to the chother. All those little distancings add up after a while till we're too debilitatingly detached from reality to meaningfully see ourselves beautifully at all. The vision of the chother challenges us to relinquish that distancing reflex, to kick the habit, to let go of that fear and to access a baseline recognition of kinship in others. *All* others. Numerous pilgrims, we come to realize, have been here before.

THEY ARE NOT "THEY"

In Louisville, Kentucky, there's a street corner with a sign commemorating one such everyday apocalypse. It's the spot on Fourth and Muhammad Ali (formerly Walnut) where the monk-writer Thomas Merton claimed to have experienced a laugh-out-loud epiphany in which he found it strangely and suddenly impossible to view passing strangers as at all random, uninteresting or, in any lasting way, separate from himself: "I was suddenly overwhelmed with the realization that I loved all those people, that they were mine and I theirs, that we could not be alien to one another even though we were total strangers. It was like waking from a dream of separateness, of spurious self-isolation." What's a monk to make of a man on the street? He ain't heavy, he's my chother. In piety, properly considered, there is no hierarchy. "The whole illusion of a separate holy existence is a dream."

Even as a monk, Merton found he too easily fell, years at a time by his own admission, for the sham of separateness. Even a life *set* apart—however it is we play at such illusions—can never ultimately *be* apart. "If only everybody could realize this! But it cannot be explained." His vocation to solitude, as he came to understand it, was not an escape from human communion, but a means to accessing, knowing and feeling it more deeply: "It is because I am one with them that I owe it to them to be alone, and when I am alone, they are not 'they' but my own self. There are no strangers! . . . If only we could see each other that way all the time." If only, but an insight can't be explained any more than it can be enforced. Like an ethic or a witness, it can only be, as it were, stumbled into, fallen upon and, in the way of the gift, received. It seems to me that Merton is describing what we might helpfully have before us now in the tale of the chother, one more variation in the age-old human solidarity song and dance. I submit it as one more song or dance to live by.

For all its profundity, the Louisville epiphany is an easier yoke, a lighter burden, than the wicked dream of self-attribution. Deliverance from the illusory difference—the positing of a *mine* that is forever and in no way *yours*—is a most serious relief, a relief that can turn the whole world around. Merton equates it with the overcoming of evil with good: "If only they could all see themselves as they really are. There would be no more war, no more hatred, no more cruelty, no more greed . . . I suppose the big problem would be that we would fall down and worship each other." Self-knowledge gives rise to right reverence of self and others. With great reverence comes great responsibility. And to call it *social* responsibility would be a redundancy, because in Merton's vision, like that of the great commandment, the false distinction between love of neighbor and love of self is collapsed. There is ultimately no such thing as a non-social self. It appears to be a work of accessing that part of us that *isn't* divided from others, that we somehow know *can't* be. The moment Merton chronicled was a realization of self—a more fully chothered self—so experientially known as the gift of mutual life that it's somehow "inaccessible to the fantasies of our own mind or the brutalities of our own will . . . the pure glory of God in us . . . our dependence." It can be glimpsed, this essential self, this divine image within everyone, this soul. Maybe even insinuated. But it won't be proven or preached. Only testified to, witnessed and proffered as a way of seeing. Only felt: "I have no program for this seeing. It is only given. But the gate of heaven is everywhere."[2]

COMPLEX REMINDINGS

Never one for flights of disembodied fancy, Merton—it seems to me—isn't spiritualizing everything so much as he's including everything in whatever we believe we've contained or cordoned off with the word *spiritual*. In this sense, heaven has nowhere else to happen but here, in the lives and bodies of those near and far. It's a call to apocalypse *now*, not at all—not even remotely—a retreat to another world, but a deeper, more intense engagement with the one we're in, the world we have, the world many witnesses have insisted God *so* loves.

Or consider it this way: "The context of love is the world."[3] Here Merton's fellow Kentuckian Wendell Berry drops an aphorism so plainly true, yet so plainly revolutionary as to merit a tattoo. The love you carry in your heart is . . . largely delusional till it puts on flesh. It simply has to. It requires a context to exist. It can't survive as theory or fantasy. It has to step out. It's the chother or nothing at all. Love requires a neighborhood. My big ideas, my alleged virtues and values, and my supposed integrity will have to be played out in the blessedly difficult, mundane sacred of where I am. This realization is lost on me repeatedly as I fall again into a dream of separateness, seemingly more manageable than the awkward fact of other people, seeming preferable to a deeper awareness of the natural world. But I'm awakened and restored to a sense of my situatedness by all manner of what Berry calls complex remindings,[4] at the center of which are experiences relayed and remembered, the images, words and analogies that make for poetry. Poetry deepens and renews my discernment of the beauty and fragility of my context—its dearness—and assures me once more that there's no escape from it. There's no outside, we might say, to the social pipeline, but poetry is that which orients me back to the joy of dwelling rightly and righteously within it, that which reminds me I'm always within it one way or another.

There's an urgency to this coming alive—or coming alive *again*—to the fact of relation, and it's captured profoundly and lastingly in a centering provocation of Hillel the Elder: "If I am not for myself, who will be for me? But if I am only for myself, who am I? If not now, when?"[5] It's as if we're being accosted by a two-millennia-old wit that knows—then *and* now—that all our deadly, self-attribution pouting is a kind of delay tactic of intensely unhelpful and even murderous denial. What am I? And who can ever reach me in my closed-up loneliness if I keep kidding myself with a false image of an isolated, self-sufficient self? I can't even *help* myself. We can fool ourselves, and we do. That which often passes for civilization and society is, in fact, ordered and organized around this delay tactic. But the rabbi calls us—and a prophetic tradition calls *through* him—to forget this house of cards. It's a farce. We can die trying, and we do. But we *cannot be* alien to one another.

The chother is the fact of the matter. We were never alone. We were all held as babies *by others*. We're likely being held—in more ways than we can even name—right now. We can live into and within the awkward-feeling fact of others, or we can die denying. Choose the chother now. The glory of God in us *is* our dependence, the fact that we can't escape the network of mutuality that makes our eating and breathing and welfare possible. Know it feelingly. Choose life. If not now, when?

Must. Let. Go.

Abstraction, we often feel, is easier—easier to quantify and less of a stumbling block to that perverse conception of dignity with which

I demand a strict sense of self-suffiency of myself and others, as if the world needs more of the delusional and desperate dance in which we try to keep up appearances. The appearance of only *minding my own business*—as if such a thing were possible—is the preferred mode in the impolite society of hyperindividualism and self-attribution. I have a story that speaks to this subject. It isn't completely flattering.

I was in San Diego impersonating—very badly—a surfer. I was completely hopeless. At the most, I could claim five solid seconds standing solidly on the board. The rest was all saltwater of the beloved Pacific, in and out of my nose for hours on end. A generous onlooker, however, might nevertheless have seen in me the signs of an excellent father. I'd swim out with my youngest son, Peter (sacred articulator of the chother principle), and offer shivering screams of support. I'd push his board—sometimes expertly on time—in anticipation of the breaking wave that would engulf me before I could recover enough to witness his totally awesome progress. No absentee parent, I.

Except I almost was absent in what was, for me, a humiliatingly definitive sense. The ritual whereby I'd cry out affirmation as we returned to each other to venture out again was interrupted by the realization that I was suddenly too far out to see or even call out to him. And with each wave, however hard I tried to plant my feet in the sand to stop moving or swim briskly and competently to the shore, I was being pulled out farther, becoming more exhausted, wondering if my movements were slipping into a panic mode (as I now know they were). And—most surprisingly to me at the time—I was preparing to let go of my sense of composure which, I came to see, was peculiarly sacred to me. Oh, how I cling to composure. *Must let go.* Surprisingly, and even disturbingly, I believe I experienced a moment in which I wondered if I was going to let go of that composure, a second or two in which I actually weighed it out and decided I would rather live having lost it than die keeping it. To name one soul who came to mind, I owed as much to my chother, my brother, my son. Don't be ridiculous, I said to myself. You need help.

"I think I need some help over here," I yelled to a nearby surfer (I *think* I need . . . ? God help me). He obliged and allowed me to clutch his board as I tried to catch my breath ("I think I just . . . need a minute"). Missing waves he wished he was catching, he rebuffed my pathetic efforts at small talk. In hindsight, I can understand his annoyance as I asked—oh so pathetically—if he was from the area.

"Here comes the lifeguard," he mumbled, disappearing without one word further as my young, able-bodied savior hugged me with a flotation device. It gets worse. Safe in my lifeguard's arms, I tried to kick a little, the better to somehow self-reassuringly carry—or appear to carry—my own weight.

"It's probably best if you just stay still," he observed politely as we took another wave together. Per regulation, it seems, he wasn't going to take the floatie off till we were both standing on the shore in plain view of everyone. Because he was off searching for me elsewhere, my son was spared the sight of his no longer indomitable dad trying to thank someone for saving his life while also looking to distance and disassociate himself as speedily as possible.

"Where were you?" he asked with wide-eyed alarm when we finally found each other.

"Have a seat on the towel," I said. "We need to talk."

WHAT'S THE MYTH?

I'm still contemplating my complex reminding. Something in my conception of myself, I believe I can say, was irretrievably—or maybe a little more definitively—undone. And it wasn't just the fantasy that, in a pinch, my stamina will somehow magically conquer any and every obstacle; that a deep adrenaline reserve will kick in so I'll have no need of anyone. It's as if a myth I thought had no hold on me to begin with—I read Wendell Berry and Thich Nhat Hanh, for God's sake—was now *really* no longer available to me. I thought I was over it. I wasn't. And—God help me—I'm not. Trying to process the experience with my daughter Dorothy a day or two later, she asked the obvious question: "What's the myth?"

I couldn't sum it up in a sentence, but it was as if I could feel my own body repenting of a certain thoughtlessness and my mind was trying to catch up with it (it still is). I felt compelled to apply the complex reminder I'd experienced immediately and widely, the better to steward the thing, to remain awake to it, to access what information my shame and frustration and bodily humiliation might have for me. I didn't want to regain my lost composure just yet. Instead, I wanted to let it remain lost for righteousness's sake, for the sake of beauty. What's the myth? The nearest example of one hidden but powerful mythology at work involved some excellently prepared chicken my daughter and I had recently shared upon purchasing it at a nearby farmer's market that day. I could start there.

There's a way of describing that particular exchange which goes like this: We paid for it with our money. So we're square. The end.

Having just had my life saved by a couple of strangers, I felt weirdly uninclined to accept that version of a recent event. It was just one more iteration of what we might call the reigning religious faith of the Western world, a uniquely unbeautiful myth, one in which the cessation of relationship occurs—split, divided, exhausted, conquered, over and done—when *I* say it does, when *I* think it's finished. It's the self-attribution fallacy all over again. Reducing the care of the chicken, the life of the chicken, the preparation of one part of a meal, the labor and care of the people behind it and our enjoyment of the whole situation to the exchange of one form of alleged currency felt somehow awkward and inappropriate. I didn't want to think that way anymore. In the wake of the waves that almost drowned me, I found that I honestly couldn't. What a waste of time such self-deception is. And to regularly insist that *this* can be reduced to *that*, in all the exchanges that make up a day, began to feel like life lived as a sort of smear campaign, life lived one *Hurry up and matter!*, one degrading myth too far. What if God remembers everything money makes us forget?[6] Maybe we can try to, too. No more bypassing the chother.

A SAVING MEMORANDUM

Why not err on the side of the relational? Why not repent of all the insidiously goofy ways we try to keep realization of community at a distance? Life's too short not to. Our life is one long process of mutual aid, and what a relief it is when people act on this knowledge. I want to keep within me and hold to the wit and the sensitivity of spirit to see, feel, appreciate, fear and revere the inescapable fact of my own caught-uppedness in the web of other people's kindness.

The fact of the chother, after all, is anything but a buzzkill. It's the hoax of a self-sufficing ego that is ultimately tiresome. I breathe better and can better enjoy a paper plate full of well-prepared chicken as an enchanted thing when I'm freed from the knee-jerk denial of the liturgy that brought it to me. We might begin to spy the possibilities of undivided living, living marked by deep integrity and humility in its root sense (*humus*, earth) of *knowingly* earth-bound life, situated and connected to the existence of everyone else; not detached, disincarnated or, in any sense, above it all, but grounded in the joys of conscious relationship. How might I proceed in my getting and doing while holding—or being held by—the realization that everything that lives is holy, life delighting in life?

The insight of my—*our*—life as chother comes to me as one more saving *memorandum* (Latin for something we will do well to remember) that protects me from the deluding abstractions that would otherwise leave me estranged, one more item of cosmic plain speak we can add to the sacred inventory that gives our speech sense to begin with. Sensible speech eschews abstraction and intensely attends to the minute particulars. Art, science and other forms of human thriving—Blake again—have nowhere to really happen, nowhere to exist save in minutely organized particulars at large somewhere. The nowhere talk of general good is the abstracting plea of scoundrels, hypocrites and flatterers. All the little distancings of generalized and commercialized life that estrange me from my neighbors—and they from me—can add up in the course of the day, distorting my self-perception so powerfully that I'm largely immunized to wisdom.

Against these perverse mental processes underlying our perverse speech, the Jesuit priest-poet Daniel Berrigan recalls that, for the prophets, there are no generalized, contextless visions, because ideas can only live in people and places and things. The prophets enact, demand and invite us to join them—as they always do—in a more subtle perception of the sweet old world.

> In the prophets, we note that "the world" is never generic; it is one's own world. It is the slow cohering over long time of a culture; friends and family and land and language and dance and song; a world of coherence and beauty, each element infinitely precious, irreplaceable. Thus "the world," a cohesion of beauty and truth and joy, makes sense, wins the heart, becomes one's own—as a dance does, a poem, a work of art. (Especially for children, that "world" in all its fragility is to be cherished and guarded, a nest in which coherence, truth, and tenderness are honored.)[7]

Oh, how we're prone to flee—in mind and body—a lived realization of the fact of our own nestedness. And what damage we wreak by doing so. The context of life and love *is* the world. Until we experience it as such, our energies know no rest and we have yet to make our home, our neighborhood, our own. No one gets to have their existence alone.

But as ever, nobody can force us to feel ourselves bound by beauty to the duty of seeing ourselves inextricably and blessedly tied to one another in all things. There can be no compulsion, after all, in religion. A lived celebration of awareness can't be coerced upon anyone. We can't be exactly be made to see ourselves in others or enter into that more direct unity of the chother. But it could be that, until we do, we have yet to assume our full humanity. I think here of Ralph Ellison's *Invisible Man*, whose narrator offers his own singular experience as one black man in a world ordered according to the rules of white supremacy in the hope that the reader might somehow sense his or her own voice in a tale candidly told, a social pipeline overlooked a thousand times, now made visible. Radically openhanded telling true, he imagines, is probably his only possible method and his only hope. "What else could I do? What else but try to tell you what was really happening when your eyes were looking through?" asks the Invisible Man. Maybe we *will* see. Perhaps a call is being successfully transmitted: "Who knows but that, on the lower frequencies, I speak for you?"[8]

With this question a table is set and a site is made ready and available for all takers. Perhaps the form of life I've tried to conjure here shall *in*form yours. Maybe it's been happening all along. And more, perhaps we aren't merely being addressed, spoken *to*; maybe we even feel we've been spoken *for*. Perhaps we hear our own voice lifted somehow within the voices of others. If not now, when?

8

Policy is liturgy writ large

How did we get so morally strange?

Teju Cole

ONCE HAD A STRANGE EXCHANGE, and it went something like this.

I stood in a driveway with the pastor of a large congregation making small talk while keeping a watchful eye on children skateboarding. There was a lull.

"I'm an advocate," he said, breaking the silence. "Wait—that's not the word." I waited for the word. "I believe in climate change," he said starting again, and I agreed that one would not want to self-identify as an advocate of climate change. "I believe in climate change, but if I told my congregation they'd probably tar and feather me." Silence. "I guess that makes me a silent prophet."

My head began to spin. There was so much I wanted to say. Prophets, we might say, are many things, but silence is not in the job description. You don't get to say nothing and be one. You can't sound a clear note and mislead simultaneously. Hide it under a bushel? No. Perhaps we should pray together that a witness might arise from within your congregation. Is it right to drive around listening to NPR while rolling your eyes over what parishioners might say if they knew you were listening to NPR? Maybe they could handle it. Maybe they're counting on you to tell them things they won't like, things they aren't hearing from anyone else they feel they can trust. Isn't there another adjective for the prophet who's silent? Is *false* the word we're looking for?

I didn't say any of these things. But the lava flowed within my heart for days. Doubtless trying to score a few righteousness points, I rambled it all off to another pastor. He smiled and dropped a helpful word on me: "Well, I guess *you* were a silent prophet then." Oh my, yes.

Compassionately skewered, I gave the matter a little more thought. It took me an embarrassingly long while, but I came to conclude that my silent prophet pastor was paying me a deep compliment. Why would he say something like that to me? Why would he entrust me with the airing out of that unflattering self-assessment?

Maybe for the same reason I set myself up to get knocked down a few days later. Maybe we can't help it. If, as ancient authority has it, we are somehow each person in our dreams, maybe something like an unconscious desire to overcome estrangement is at work in the things we say without knowing why. Given what he took to be my commitments (I am, as you can see by now, a bit of a talker), my pastor friend was actually kind enough to wonder what I might have to say to the fact that he has yet to share his conviction concerning the future of the planet with his congregants who—perhaps sometimes aggressively—don't. Every spoken word is an act of faith, after all, but there I stood missing my cue, opting out for a separate, holier-than-thou existence, missing the fact of my nearby chother asking for a little input. Judging feels easier and stronger than empathy sometimes. It isn't.

It's a complicated business bearing witness. So many compromises in the space of one day. So many opportunities to drop the ball of being true. So many supposedly solid reasons to live just short of full disclosure in our communications with people (associates? friends? sisters? brothers? congregants?) who might be surprised to hear how unsafe we presume they'd prove to be were we to do something as radical as, say, make the fullness of our alleged convictions known. Dare we attempt courtesy of the heart in our everyday dealings? Do we dare, in the parlance of gambling and law enforcement, show our hands?

If our vocation, our deepest calling, is to ring true, and if our witness is the sum of everything we do, we might begin to conclude that life's too short not to. I know it's complicated, but maybe we owe it to our chother to come out of hiding as often as possible. Why must we front with one another? Every ancient prophecy assures us *truth will out* anyway. And yes, it's hard to understand something when our paycheck depends on not understanding it, but what does it profit a prophet to gain a world of popular credibility and forfeit the will and the wit to say what's plainly true? It's always been a hard pill to swallow, but what else are gospel, prophecy and poetry for? They're here to set what is captive free. Another day,

> **Maybe we owe it to our chother to come out of hiding as often as possible.**

another opportunity to repent of idolatrous thinking. Another chance to convert and to come clean. I have in mind the long conversion only relationship—a deep awareness of the chother—can nurture. Are we up for the risk?

To be whole is to be part. None of us gets to have our meaning alone. We can't ultimately escape the living fact of our relationship to others. At our best, we know it and celebrate it instead of denying it recognition the way our postures and power drives make us think we have to. Or as the mystic practitioner of Public Broadcasting, Fred Rogers, once put it, as if calling to us from an alternate universe, "We are intimately related. May we never even pretend that we are not." But pretend we do, and our pretense costs the whole of creation dearly. True religion necessitates the showing of hands, and when we don't, we do endless damage to every minute particular. Love's labor's lost again and again. The silences that surround the fact of global warming, the everyday social tragedy we bankroll in our soul-flaying commitment to mass incarceration and the human sacrifices we exact under the banner of our supposed security aren't random; they're orchestrated. To borrow Octavia Butler's phrase, we are the ordinary people who fund and underwrite the monstrous things our society sanctions as legal and proper. How might we begin to overcome the ugly ordering of our worlds?

"The revolt against brutality begins with a revolt against the language that hides that brutality."[1] This is Rebecca Solnit with a very helpful aphorism concerning the way we kid ourselves with words, the speech habits that roll in and out of the mental habits at work in our perverse ordering of bodies, communities and resources. As Jesus insists, it's the way we speak that defiles us. To conceive of religion under the dictation of popular headlines is to conceive it incoherently. To perceive it as somehow separate from the whole of human behavior is to hide from ourselves. We have to think before we can make sense. Newspeak touts "the role of religion," people *getting* religion, "religious issues" or the presence of a "religious aspect" in the interest of presenting a "religious angle." This is like saying—as if it were a compellingly interesting news item—that "Relationship was a factor," "Language played a role" or "Culture was involved." But the fact is it's always already there. It can't suddenly enter the picture. We can't get past religion any more than we can live without communal ties, societies, stories or symbols. It's what we're up to. It is, in so many ways, the human subject.

We're always consecrating in one way or another, and my religion—if it's to be true, if it's to be faithful, life-giving and responsible to the possibility of life, will have to take the form of a question. What does my witness actually consist of?

EVERYDAY LITURGIES

Like our religion, our liturgy (*leitourgia*, the work of the people) is never more nor less than what we actually do with our energies. And when we try to divide up the world in such a way that a suicide bombing is *religiously* motivated but the crowd killing of alleged anonymous militants in a drone strike, for instance, is borne of the *always reasonable* demands of national security, we leave dysfunctional orderings of human life, the bad religion we underwrite with our getting and spending, our voting, our tax dollars and our consuming unchallenged. We let ourselves off the hook when we imagine we can keep any behavior outside of the sphere of our alleged religious commitments,

> **All religion, all the time.**

the stories to which we pledge our allegiance whether consciously or unconsciously with everything we do and don't do. All religion—repeat after me if you're willing and able—all the time. All religion, all the time.

This returns us to the question of our attention collections as the way our specific lives specifically play out in an attention economy, the everyday liturgies we perpetuate in the minute particulars. If religion names the ordering of our priorities, what miracles might come when we begin to pay attention to ourselves? What conversions might wakefulness require? If, as *myth*ing persons, we never outgrow our need for a coherent account, a better story of what we've experienced and what we're up to, how might we tell *and live* a better one, one more intensely concerned with and responsive to the life of the world? How might we live divided no longer?

I believe we begin by exercising certain duties of resistance when it comes to the stories we sponsor and sustain—they're religions, after all—when we go with the flow to the detriment of our world, our neighborhood, and to the detriment of other people living and yet to be born. There is no moment in which you are not mattering, belonging in one way or another, living up to or in general contempt of any number of narrow or incredibly broad traditions. It is sometimes said that it's the narrower ones that lead to life. How's your traditioning coming along? Whatever the currents are that move you, they're flowing—it's perhaps helpful to observe—right now. Your religion is the story you tell yourself about yourself to others. As it happens, it doesn't always coincide with what we think—or say—we believe.

Will it turn out that you belonged mostly uncritically and unthinkingly to a particular cultural context? Did you wrestle with it or was your life one of automatic obedience, a series of unfortunate events in which you carefully ascertained what values you were expected to appear to have from one moment to the next and dutifully did so, aping along as it were along the path of least resistance? Were you, in large part, a silent prophet?

BAD RELIGION BREAKS THE WORLD

Like worship, liturgy or even faith, it seems to me that there is no off switch in these matters. It's horribly unpoetic, but this insight might also serve us well in coping with a phrase I'm accustomed to hearing with strange frequency: value system. Like "human resources," it's an oddly perverse saying, but maybe it's one more way of naming the raw feed of all we're up to as individuals, communities, countries and those combined collective efforts of extraction, sales and consent called corporations. Value systems—the values we actually embody, *not* the values we say we have or try to *advertise* ourselves as having—are glaringly, sometimes crushingly obvious. All day long, nonstop, we value and devalue people, places, things and the possibility of arable land and potable water for the babies to come. "What shall we value today?" we get to ask ourselves each morning. What minute particulars will I fix my attention upon? Who and what do I mean to love well? Your gift to the world might be answering these questions well from time to time, pulling this one off in your own small way with your own set of sensitivities and enthusiasms, taking the measure of your own attention span, which is, of course, a kind of prayer. To ring true, to sound your one clear note with your one life . . . might it be appropriate to kind of think of it as something like your duty, dharma or the word of God to you?

If it's right to say that my values are being visually systematized in all that I say and do, I begin to see that I have more avenues for faithfulness, for life and liveliness, than the conventional dividing up of reality allows for. I have a couple of aphorisms I find it helpful to keep in front of me as I try to overcome the false dichotomies coming at me in every form of teleprompter, damaging dualisms which, unless I resist them, I find deeply imprinted in my thinking, my speech and my everyday imagination. The first is from Irenaeus of Lyon: The glory of God is a human being fully alive. The second is my own: Policy is liturgy writ large.

These two are aphorisms enough to problematize—righteously problematize?—all manner of issues; certainly more than I can count. But at the risk of inspiring issue fatigue, I'd like us to consider some questions they generate: What might we gain if we begin to consider climate change, immigration, health care, waste disposal, foreign policy and the right to clean water as ineluctably religious issues? What do we lose when we refuse to? If we refuse to recognize our own religiosity, our own complicity, in the living out of very bad ideas about the world, our costly complacency goes unchecked. We need not look too far to see and know—feelingly know—the ways our bad religion breaks the world. We dwell in the fact of its establishment. We always have.

To the issue of government-sponsored terror—whether involving Muslims tortured, detained and killed without trial, the escalation of drone strikes, or, in Charles Krauthammer's perverse phrase, "telegenically dead"[2] Palestinians—the novelist Teju Cole recently raised an especially poignant plea: "How did we get so morally strange?"[3] While I imagine there's no end to possible responses to this colossal question, the one with the most gravitational pull in my thinking is the popular bracketing off of religion—faith, liturgy, common life—from the violence our society normalizes in the name of perceived necessity. True religion knows no neat divisions. The more we divide the less we see.

Everyday Idolatries

"I was in danger of verbalizing my moral impulses out of existence."[4] Anybody know the feeling? These are the words—I wish they were more well-known—of one of my favorite realists in the world. In a wonderfully specific way they name the danger we're all in, but they were uttered in the context of a criminal trial. It's Daniel Berrigan I'm talking about. Let me explain.

We heard from Father Berrigan in the preceding chapter concerning a prophetic understanding of the world—the world God so loves, the world that is our home and the world for which we are, all of us, in so many ways responsible, the world that is our gift, our inheritance and our trust. As a poet and a priest for whom the entire world, down to the minutest particular, is charged with the grandeur of God, he views the cosmos as a space in which there are no unrelated phenomena and tries to live accordingly. And like so many in our beleaguered times, Berrigan is involved in a mental struggle, a moral improvisation when it comes to the question of how to dwell redemptively in an age gone mad, an age largely in thrall to the social dictates of, if I may be permitted an awkward mouthful, the military-industrial-entertainment-incarceration complex. Berrigan, as ever, describes the dysfunction, this mess wrought by all manner of misconceived human self, more poetically: "Immortal urges do not come cheap, whether in lives or resources."[5]

In the course of his long life, Berrigan has served for and within many a community of discernment around the world as an intellectually lyrical presence in speaking justly to power and figuring out what faithfulness looks like in the shadow of our reigning geopolitical liturgies of domination and degradation. While he's clearly felt the pinch in different ways throughout the decades, the season in which he articulated this concern over verbalizing his moral impulses into nonexistence was at the height of the Vietnam War in the late sixties. His late brother and fellow Jesuit Philip Berrigan, a combat veteran of World War II whom civil rights activist Stokely Carmichael once described as "the only white man who knows where it's at,"[6] had been involved in various mass actions throughout the era, but Daniel had mostly expressed opposition to the war in classrooms and in writing. For both Berrigans, the extent to which the alleged leadership of churches throughout North America had obediently lined up to support uncritically the United States government's endless military escalation had given rise to a vocational crisis. Where was the witness to the gospel of God's righteous kingdom? Where was the church? Where was Jesus? As Daniel put the question:

> Who owned the tradition, anyway; and who was worthy to speak on its behalf? . . . Indeed, the issue was not simply that a tradition was traduced daily by those responsible for its purity and truth. The issue was a far more serious one. . . . The tradition was a precious voice, a presence, a Person. The war had silenced the voice, outlawed the Person. Church and state had agreed, as they inevitably did in time of war, that the

Person was out of fashion, "for the duration." He had nothing
to offer in the face of guns. . . . He was a prisoner of war this
Jesus. He was in a species of protective custody.[7]

What were they to do when so many in their own communities had
largely reduced themselves to radio silence? How were they to keep
their vows to be ambassadors of God's righteous order without
publicly protesting—in some demonstrative way—the idolatrous
ordering of the nation-state? They would bring the liturgical forms
with which they'd been entrusted by their tradition to the war-
making liturgies, the paperwork, for instance, of the United States
government whose enlisting of young men to commit acts of indis-
criminate violence and devastation upon the people and the land
of Vietnam constituted, according to their understanding of
Scripture, a demonic stronghold. Following much prayer and weeks
of discussion, on May 17, 1968, they joined seven other activists and
walked into a draft board in Catonsville, Maryland, removed papers
with the names of men scheduled to be conscripted and conducted
the prayerful burning of draft files with homemade napalm. Apolo-
gizing for their fracture of what they could no longer abide as "good
order," and noting that they were no longer able to say "Peace, peace"
when there is no peace, they observed that they thought it fitting
to burn paper instead of children: "We could not, so help us God,
do otherwise." As the fire burned, they punctuated this purposeful
ritual by reciting the Lord's Prayer.

They viewed their action as a redemptive raid on the *sacrosanct*.
And a moment's reflection on that almost excruciatingly helpful
adjective—sacrosanct—is a reminder that it is indeed *ever in play*:
borders, weapons facilities, private property, bodies, laptops, art
installations, automobiles, wildlife preserves, smartphones, paper
money, documents, designated areas. Choose your own liturgy?
We do. All the time. And the Catonsville Nine did one fine day:

"Those draft files! They were, of course, more than they purported to be. They had an aura, they were secular-sacred documents of the highest import."[8] They chose to be militantly transparent—maybe life's too short not to—when it counted. And in this way, their *transparent* liturgy would serve to disrupt and destabilize, even if only in one neighborly instance, the *unacknowledged* liturgy of the draft. Were they wrong to do so? Our answer will largely depend on our sense of the sacrosanct. What's yours? Take your time on that one; it's difficult to discern the content of your own religion. But it's worth trying to find out.

THE ACTUAL WORLD IS OUR ONLY WORLD

What did they accomplish? They went to jail, their faces were placed on the cover of *Time* magazine, their criminalized behavior was a *palpable hit* in the sense that it *made the news* for a time. Similar actions they and others undertook and which continue into our day, often under the moniker of the Plowshares Movement, pose, as the prophetic always does, the question of authority. To whom and what are we rightly *subject*? What shall we *credit*? How shall we *adhere*? To what are we *devoted*? Like any prophets in any era we care to name, the Catonsville Nine confronted and dramatized the reigning dysfunction of their day in one specific and costly way. By confronting and dramatizing American liturgy at home and abroad, the action sought to provoke a meaning crisis for the American public, positing a sacred sense of reality counter to reigning disorder, making plain the brutal arbitrariness of "the way things are," creating scenes of recognition in which the habitual devaluing of life is no longer deemed inevitable, necessary or even realistic. As Daniel Berrigan modestly puts it, the poor mortal is to go ahead in spite of all:

> I tried, in response, to put matters biblically. That there was a history for acts such as ours. In such biblical acts, results,

outcome, benefits, are unknown, totally obscure. The acts are at variance with good manners and behavior. Worse, they are plainly illegal. More yet: everything of prudence and good sense points to the uselessness and ineffectiveness of such acts. . . . And yet, and yet, it is also said: The poor mortal is to go ahead; in spite of all. To go ahead, in faith; which is to say, because so commanded. . . . One had very little to go on; and went ahead nonetheless. Still, the "little," I reflected ruefully, had at least one advantage. One was free to concentrate on the act itself, without regard to its reception in the world. Free also to concentrate on moral preparation, consistency, conscience. Looked at in this light, the "little" appeared irreducible, a treasure. . . . So, despite all, a history of sorts was launched on a May morning in 1968. Also, a tradition was vindicated, at least to a degree. Or so I believe to this day.[9]

There is so much here. So many evocative phrases, so many possible album/novel/book-of-poetry titles: A History of Sorts, Everything of Prudence and Good Sense, Very Little to Go On. "Very little to go on" is the one that brings to mind W. H. Auden's everlasting take on the paradoxical power of the poetic as that which makes nothing *happen* and yet survives somehow in the valley of having been said, however seemingly ineffectively, a way of happening; a way of happening that might be just gentle and precise enough to change everything. In this case, the seemingly weak gesture was, for the Berrigans, nothing less than the vindication *in time*, the public coherence outside one federal building in 1968, of the biblical tradition itself. Nine supposed nobodies gave witness to it, after all, in the space of minutes, speaking the truth in love one more time, standing by the jams, the redemption songs of millennia. The popular news cycle paid heed within hours, but one on-the-scene verification came immediately from a local FBI agent who upon seeing Philip exclaimed, "Him again! Good God, I'm changing my religion!" The liturgical clarification had gotten through. As Daniel saw it, "I could think of no greater tribute to my brother."[10]

The befuddled and frustrated law enforcement officer is not alone in his confusion. Isn't the church supposed to stay out of politics? Isn't all that deeply comforting mumbo jumbo all about the next life? Against that best-selling false witness that strictly concerns itself primarily with otherworldly consolation, Berrigan posits that the biblical vision is one in which "the actual world is our only world,"[11] and insists that divinity—God's good purposes—must be understood as operative in the this-worldly, reality-based realm. Berrigan's biblical thinking insists that *now* is the new *then*. According to his long career of living witness, it's what the God who is love, the love that is and was and is to come, is for:

> Humankind, it seems, has always been overdue to see God's Word as subversive of a human dis-order largely disobedient, rebellious, and perverted—one close to self-destruction from toxic fouling of our nest, or from weapons designed to protect our *mammon*, the money of exploitation. The word of God revolutionizes this social chaos nonviolently, replacing the politics of greed, blood lust, and violence with politics designed for children.[12]

And with this appeal to A. J. Muste's famous demand—still largely unmet—for a foreign policy dedicated to the healthy thriving of children, the pervasive moral strangeness we breathe and normalize with our everyday acquiescence is once again brought to light. Then as now, we forget so easily. Like so much human goodness, the Berrigan witness often seems to have been forgotten or repressed. But oftentimes, when I mention the names of Daniel and Philip Berrigan to American men of a certain age, I see a light go on in their faces as if they're waking from a dream or recollecting a moment of clarity that once resonated most decisively before life moved on. They're the men who once waited to see when their number might come up. Many went overseas and some stayed in school to avoid the draft, found employment that would exempt them, fled the country or, as is the case with more than a few, watched certain strings get pulled to keep them out of harm's way. They remember those priests who practiced what they preached by throwing a wrench in the machinery of death, by bearing witness to a universal and transcendent life in a dark time. For a good many people, it was a very big deal. For David Byrne—yes, David Byrne of the Talking Heads—it was a godsend. A Maryland resident at the time, he recalled that his own name was likely among those listed in that sacrosanct paperwork made to go up in smoke.[13] He remains thankful for the way those nine people struck a human note that was heard around the world—at least for a little while. Maybe you are too.

What's Your Name?

So do we have the Catonsville Nine to thank for the existence of the Talking Heads among us? I'd say definitely maybe. We can perhaps more conclusively conclude that one feat of attentiveness leads to another and that the world gets turned around one act of neighborliness at a time. Given the relative obscurity of the Berrigan witness in popular memory now and how far we are these days from their plainspoken proclamation of God's order over everyday human disorder, we might wonder as well how it is that we've come to expect so little of people who call themselves Christian.

I should note that it's taken me a while to see and accept—and I'm never done seeing and accepting—that a move so seemingly radical as that of the Catonsville Nine is par for the course for communities that mean to seek right perception and right relationship in a hypermilitarized and hypermonetized world. When I was twenty-two years old and not many years past my Kroger parking lot epiphany, I had a degree of awareness concerning the existence of such communities, but there remained many a dot that I had yet to see connected.

It was the summer of 1992, and having ferried and hitchhiked over from a YMCA outdoor center where I lived and worked in Northern Ireland, I sat in an enormous tent at the Greenbelt Arts Festival at Castle Ashby where I listened to the priest-professor Henri Nouwen teach and pray and expound upon his vision of the life of the spirit lived in community. I reveled in his description of spiritual discipline, Jesus' own need for solitude and his stories of life with Jean Vanier and the members of the L'Arche community. But I was tripped up when, toward the end, a story of his time among the impoverished of Peru rolled into an indictment of the United States government's role in paramilitary violence in Guatemala, El Salvador and Nicaragua. I didn't see what the one had to do with the other, and my own sense of reality at the time was, I'll admit, unduly influenced by the hours I'd clocked in as an avid listener of the radio personality Rush Limbaugh.

I'm not sure what I had in mind, but I somehow felt the need— defensively minded young person that I was—to let him know that humanity's definition of justice might not always coincide with the true, pristine, real, capital "J" Justice of God, that we mustn't presume. So I intercepted his exit, introduced myself and mumbled my way through whatever it was I wanted to say as my enthusiasm quickly outran my verbal coherence.

"And what's your name again?" he asked with a smile and a steadfast refusal to remove his eyes from mine.

Flustered: "Um. David."

"Hello, David," he intoned in an alarmingly unhurried fashion. Nouwen then proceeded to ask me numerous questions about where I was from, how I'd found myself there, and all this with a generous commentary (leading to further questions) on all my responses. He'd stopped dead in his tracks and didn't seem at all inclined to be on his way until I'd had enough. Before I knew it, I felt somehow simultaneously bigger, calmed, relieved of a burden and very much lifted to the height of a peer. I didn't feel knocked down by his words—that was, of course, what was really going on—any longer. Before I knew it, *I* was ready to let *him* go and did.

After he'd taken a few steps to be on his way, he turned around to say, "Oh. And what you said about justice—you're right."

I'm told that dignity isn't something you can give somebody. It's only something you can be kind or sensible enough to recognize, because people have it already, in and about themselves, whether we choose to realize it or not. It's in them even when they don't know it. And maybe we feel it most solidly in ourselves when someone's decided to act or speak in deep recognition of its presence. Nouwen made me feel my own dignity, and it was as if I was being inaugurated into the way of the gift and invited, once again, into a community of sanity marked by what the apostle Paul refers to as "humility of mind."

Such humility comes most naturally to us when we're possessed by a sense of righteous abundance and the better ordering of life it demands. If we think of it as an order to which we're invited to pay heed in all we say, do and conceive, it's also a righteous abundance in which we find and lose ourselves all at once. It demands consistent acknowledgement of the seriousness and affection and interest with which God, we are told, regards every human being who ever lived. It could lead a person to burn a few deadly pieces of paper or respond unanxiously to an anxious interrogator or seek reconciliation with someone who's murdered someone you love. Each day is an opportunity to bring a depth charge of righteousness to any interaction. If not now, when?

I wouldn't want to single Nouwen out unhelpfully, because such gestures of love and interest had happened to me a number of times before and have continued to happen many times since. But it seems clear to me that what passed between us—or what Nouwen graciously passed over to me—was a sense of holiness. I believe holiness blooms and blossoms when we hear and heed, in our hurry and our weakness, in our depression and disinterestedness, the command to love others as we hope to be loved. It is by way of such holiness that a community of sanity is formed. Maybe it's as nearby as the nearest person who wishes someone would ask her a question.

9

Strange negotiations

We flipped a coin, okay? You and me. You and me! Coin flip is sacred.

Jesse Pinkman to Walter White in *Breaking Bad*

OFFER UP A PECULIARLY INTENSE understatement when I note that not everything that passes for church in our time could be rightly called a community of sanity, but this doesn't mean that the call to try to be one together with others is any less crucial, urgent or immediately needful. Eugene Peterson puts it provocatively and helpfully when he observes, "I don't think there's any problem with the church these days except all these *non*-churches." No problem save the plain old fact of too few people committed to trying to think and live sanely and therefore righteously together with others, come what may. Is there still a living witness among the living?

I certainly think so. I see them everywhere, actually, and I place the person, the image, the direct action, the novel, the joke, the poem, the film or the lyric in my attention collection whenever I find one. And church itself might be helpfully construed as the very community hell-bent on finding, reciting, handing down and living up to what we might yet find to be of help in the life's work of thinking and living sanely . . . or *in*sanely, depending upon who's passing judgment. That which constitutes life and righteousness is often foolishness to the powers that be. The poet Fanny Howe is especially eloquent concerning the countercultural realism to which those who seek true religion are called: "You know that we all, no matter what we do, answer to the time we were born in. We *are* the time we inhabit. . . . This is the interesting part of being Catholic: The heresy that comes along with it. Indistinguishable from the rites is the rage, the arguing, the rebelling, the mind on alert. I like to be on alert. And I like to be in an atmosphere where people examine one more completely insane vision of the universe."[1]

A mind on alert won't settle for the deadly divides that destroy neighbor, neighborhood and planet, and a mind on alert won't accept that the way things are is the way things have to be. The mind on alert is committed to overcoming every death-dealing division with the living out of prophetic consciousness in all matters. The

> **A mind on alert won't accept that the way things are is the way things have to be.**

fact of the reigning dysfunction wherever we turn is simply a call for renewed examination and a determined leaning in as we dream up better ways of conceiving our relationship to others. May we never be incurious when it counts. Maybe it always counts.

REALISTS OF A LARGER REALITY

The extraordinarily insightful essayist and chronicler of the Occupy movement, Nathan Schneider, describes the situation thus: "The circumstances of our world exceed the politics we're used to imagining for it."[2] Against the despair of the status quo, there remain so many vantage points for imagining the world more truly—that would be true religion—and for overturning the violent divisons with which we find ourselves unwittingly playing along. What alternatives to everyday despair remain unseen and untapped? What would it look like to not be forever on the run from awareness of complications?

Ursula Le Guin recently named the good work to be done with rare wit on the occasion of receiving the Medal for Distinguished Contribution to American Letters. In the face of certain perceived inevitabilities, we get to try to be people who counter—in word and deed—the reigning hypnosis: "We live in capitalism, its power seems inescapable—but then, so did the divine right of kings." Take *that*, status quo. There's more: "Any human power can be resisted and changed by human beings." If we listen hard enough, we can hear the voices of people—they really are everywhere, though they're mostly not famous—who "can see alternatives to how we live now and can see through our fear-stricken society and its ob-sessive technologies to other ways of being, and even imagine some real grounds for hope. . . . [Those] who can remember freedom— poets, visionaries—realists of a larger reality."[3]

Oh, the realists of the larger reality! Oh, I want to be in that number! Oh, to be among those—on a trajectory *with* those—who proceed sanely in word and deed. There remain before us so many avenues to social creativity, to problematizing the sad old, same old reigning nomenclatures with socially disruptive newness. Whenever we undertake this newness, whether in public or in secret, we manage, in Daniel Berrigan's phrase, to seed something into history.[4]

The alternative is crushingly familiar. We sing of love for God and weep over the wonders of God's grace while destroying land and poisoning water. Our elected leaders add to the escalating law-lessness they once promised to rectify, carefully saying whatever they think they have to say and voting however they think they have to vote to continue to hold on to their supposed power and influence. We lay waste to neighbors near and far in the name of that oft de-monic misnomer, homeland security. "The greater a hypocrisy," essayist and artist Jaron Lanier decrees, "the more invisible it typically becomes."[5] But it seems to me that if we hope to resist, counter and name these liturgies of murderous abstraction, we have to render visible—and be alive to—the social fact of religion. Doing so might be one of the nearest means we have for really facing the facts. Because every fact is a function of relationship.

Poets Are the Most Specific People on Earth

In this work, it seems to me that Daniel Berrigan might be our most eloquent diagnostician of inherited dysfunction, those religious forms that enslave all the more deviously for going unscrutinized. Here, he seems to have in mind all the trappings of officialdom and expertise, whether in courthouses, board meetings or situation rooms, and their subtle—but not so subtle—bindings. His sense of the loss of prophetic consciousness in these environments, of the way access requires that it be left at the door, is devastating:

It is necessary above all to be concrete when we speak of these things. Men, even good men, are commonly disposed to submit to the slavery of the actual; they literally cannot imagine themselves in any life situation other than the one in which they live. They inherit a style, a culture, a religion—and they prolong such forms—because they are there; useful, comfortable, logical, venerable. Their minds wear the costumes of their ancestors, a clothing that was once befitting, literally, but is now simply a folklore or a fakeout. So they call folklore a religion and a fakeout in adult life. And, alas, who shall disenchant them? But let it at least be said, as the Lord implies from His Roman courtroom, such lives as these must not make large claims to the truth.[6]

"What *is* truth?" Pontius Pilate asks Jesus in what appears to be a tone of mercenary cynicism, as if the very question is distasteful and impolitic and beneath the interest of those who matter. Who has *time* to be true anymore anyway? Why not play it safe and stick to the handed-down commands of the teleprompter? The always-alternative poetic demand a prophet like Berrigan makes of us is, for starters, to begin to find our mythological presumptions presumptuous by being awake to them. For Berrigan, this connecting of dots in the face of prevailing mythologies whose caretakers busy themselves in (and derive their status from) making sure such connections *aren't* made is the name of the human game in the worlds we're in.

Of Berrigan, Kurt Vonnegut once made the following claim: "For me Father Berrigan is Jesus as a poet. If this be heresy, make the most of it."[7] Let's do. The vocation Vonnegut spies in Brother Daniel is the one Berrigan sees in Jesus as that figure of the divine who is also, if it helps to conceive him this way, the most realistic human being who ever lived: "Jesus, by a method that was breathtakingly realistic and right, sought to break the universal dominion of Death over [women and] men."[8] The poetic-prophetic imagination that counts Jesus the Christ is, in this sense, a demythologizing force ever at work upon the prevailing, death-dealing mythologies that otherwise have their way on and in our lives to our seemingly endless detriment.

When we think of it this way, the culture we call poetry is human seriousness itself. It's the work of making all things new, redeeming the time and bodying forth newness of life and living and social possibility. With perhaps such visions in mind, the poet Anthony Towne, who, with William Stringfellow, harbored Daniel Berrigan following the Catonsville action and up until his arrest, remarked, "It is my considered opinion that any society that locks up priests is sick, and any society that imprisons poets is doomed."[9] Against the prevailing delusions of our days, the poets, those realists of a larger reality, remind us of what, in the most life-giving sense, "normal living" requires. "If there is any love in it," normal living "is one long

gorgeous and, no doubt, subversive conspiracy."[10] Larger-reality
realists are our poet-practitioners who would instruct us all in
being better caretakers of words, of what we do with words (consider, for a moment, all the wonderful and horrible things we do
with words). In this sense, theirs is the work of social mindfulness,
"Poets . . . are the most specific people on earth."[11]

KNOW THE SIZE OF YOUR VEHICLE

To think of realism in *this* way is to begin to live in the midst of all
manner of difficult questions, but I would argue that this has always
been the very joy set before us. The call to own our own religiosity—
to confess it, to repent of it and to change our ways of thinking and
living—is one with the call to love our neighbors as if they are ourselves, *because they are.* Every ancient and wise authority assures
us this is the case. And yet, this same deep joy is a deep threat—or
perceived as one—by interests that prefer to keep accounts of
people, events and doings liturgically *un*related and boundaried up.
According to the prevailing delusions, to see all human activity as
religious is to see the world illegally.[12] There are countless reasons
to keep the world divided, to not *say* what we *see* and to settle for
being silent prophets. But what if the reigning divisions are un-
wieldy *because* they're idolatrous, because they never actually serve
human interest? I would argue that, in these matters, there is
neither separation nor the possibility of critical detachment. Our
inescapable network of mutuality—our common existence—is a
living fact that can't be reasonably denied.

But in our feverish and defensive commitment to compartmen-
talization, deny it we do. By drawing a line between our supposed
convictions and our actual practices, we hold and exercise power
without taking responsibility for it. But what we believe *is* what we
do. Our policies and our liturgies are one and the same. In the case
of the United States, for instance, our neuroses reach across the

world with tragic consequences. As the journalist Mark Danner observed of the American public's responsibility in light of the disclosures of the Senate Torture Report, our fear and ignorance is translated into someone else's pain.[13] My perverse imagination is someone else's social disaster. And when it comes to the complications—the reverberations—of my getting, spending, voting and consuming, my existence is revealed to be a series of strange negotiations of which I'm only occasionally conscious.

The phrase "strange negotiations" comes to me from singer-songwriter David Bazan, who's blessed us with an album and a song by that name. An exceedingly conscientious person in sentence and song, his good humor is compellingly intertwined with a determination to look hard at societal failures that are communal failures and that are also, of course, personal failures, and his music bears his witness out in chronicles of joy and grief and self-deprecation. It's as if he's never met a survival strategy or a coping mechanism he can't figure out how to lyricize.

Of a piece with all of this is a moment I witnessed when I was with Bazan in a van as he negotiated the busy streets of Nashville. While wanting to leave town in time to reach his next venue, he also wanted to give his van-full of violinists—the Passenger String Quartet—the chance to wash their clothes in a laundromat. With OxiClean detergent balls at the ready, he had just enough time to drop them off to see to their laundry before heading for another joint.

Enter an oversized sport-utility vehicle trying to parallel park in slow, grating and very nonexpert fashion. We waited. And without forgetting that there was a real, living person in the big and inconvenient truck, Bazan allowed himself some words in a quietly exhaled plea: "Know the size of your vehicle, man."

It seems to me that there's a hungering and thirsting after righteousness in this expression, whether spoken unto ourselves or others, an invitation to take stock and to level with ourselves concerning the scope of what we're up to. I file it next—maybe it's a counterweight—to the notorious saying, "Mistakes were made," that eerie disavowal of the fact of my own doings and nondoings. We abdicate responsibility for the space we take up when we speak of decisions or actions as phenomena that occur apart from us. We also miss the good fruit that is the righteous yield of repentance, because repentance can't function as a side issue or a momentary pause after which we get swiftly back to business. To treat it as such is to deprive it of its life-giving, world-repairing power. Like grace, it gets to inform the whole of a life, every minute particular, if we're to know joy and the root of joy or be delivered from suffering and the root of suffering.

Perhaps there's a joy available to us in realizing we can't successfully separate ourselves from our chother, however it is we've sought to alleviate our anxieties. We don't finally get away with anything. Our existence simply will not be zoned off into separate sections. Maybe, at our core, we don't desire separation to begin with. Maybe we just thought we couldn't handle a vision of wholeness. Maybe all the excess complexity we mistook for chaos is actually good news. Maybe it's gospel.

More than a little bit in sync with the magnanimous, sacramental wit we spy in an artist like James Joyce, Daniel Berrigan and his ilk invite us to live in search of "the larger yes," the wider human affirmation that is often elusive but also often scandalously present in any given circumstance. We are invited, in all things, to "undertake an ethic of resurrection, and live according to the slight edge of life over death." What's resurrection? Exemplary Catholic that he is, Berrigan defines resurrection as "the hope that hopes on."[14]

WHAT DO WE VALUE?

When it comes to such an ethic, this larger yes, this seizing of that slight edge of life over death, the Berrigan witness, exemplary as I believe it to be, is, of course, just the tip of the iceberg, or *a tip* among *many* icebergs. But I admit the Berrigan standard often serves as the standard by which I judge my own canon a suitable canon, one that fits the facts as I understand them, that makes my attention collection a collection worth sharing. The Berrigans reside among various voices I depend on to keep me from abstracting myself out of the life of the world. The name Berrigan sets me to thinking, sets me to wondering how I might be more thorough in the way I'm living my life, the manner in which I'm conceiving others. And more than any figure I can think of, he reminds me— and it's often a bit of a haunting—that I'm never not being religious.

A haunting, I say, because there's many a strange negotiation in trying to be true, many a denial I'm apt to indulge in order to avoid the shame spiral that beckons when I note the distance between my big talk and my actual doings, my beliefs about myself and my general inaction. This, I suppose, is religion, the prickly, high-drama question of what it is I really value. What's more interesting and entertaining and laughable than that? Can it get any more humiliating?

One of the deep thrills of the *Breaking Bad* television series is the way it lays this question bare in the lives of high school science teacher Walter White and his former student Jesse Pinkman. In their partnership of methamphetamine production, everything begins, persists, twists and ends as the means to some supposed, seemingly inarguably good end. All manner of horror is justified by having been done (it *had* to be done) for the right reasons. Absolute security in theory, we find, leads to everyday nihilism in practice. The joys of honest speech become intensely unavailable. And it's all ... so ... familiar. They hedge. They deny. They blame. But decisions *have* to made, certain roles *have* to be played. Who'll *take care* of the situation? Who'll do the deed? In their division of labor, there's a new dilemma—sometimes many overlapping dilemmas—in every episode. Bond, from one harried moment to the next, is king. And as it is in our own lives, except even more so, for Walter and Jesse it's always a question of what they're willing to credit as binding. Propelled by perceived necessity, they will be bound to certain murderous acts. In one such instance, an agreed-upon coin toss leaves the task to Walt. Walt balks. Jesse recites the improvised creed, "We flipped a coin, okay? You and me. You and me!" And in a kind of desperate growl, "Coin flip is sacred."

It can take the edge off to see and hear yet one more sacred designation described so plainly and tragicomically, but we're kidding ourselves if we detach ourselves entirely from the strange negotiations of Jesse and Walt. We're all in it. And for many of us, it's as if we're never not monetizing, never not forcibly forgetting our interdependence for fear it'll slow us down, never not worshiping in one way or another (coin flip is sacred!). Not everyone takes the Macbeth-like path of Walter White, whose desire for complete autonomy so narrows his sphere of the sacrosanct that there's hardly anything in it save his own will to power. But most of us eschew the minute particulars in the name of security and control, forgetting—again and again—that the little things *are* the big things. So much of our energy is devoted to the externalizing of responsibility. We reach out, as the saying goes, but in our haste, our sadness and our fear, we often lose the ability to be present to one another. High drama everywhere. The little distancings, we find, add up over time. But maybe the realizations and confessions and blessed breakdowns do too.

As it turns out, we're awash in complex reminders which, if we have ears to hear and eyes to see, reveal again that the abstractions of success, progress, power and stability are not unambivalent indices. Upon examination, we will often find that the doings, policies and investments that occur beneath them are, in fact, social evils, cult activities we come to find we can no longer approve lest we conspire in the degradation and diminishment of self and neighbor. There are multiple signs everywhere—I've tried to chronicle a few in these pages—which expose and critique these unexamined liturgies. And there is that within us that is drawn to anything that invites us to acknowledge the sham, anything that facilitates the realization that so many of our perceived have-tos, the faulty blueprints we've been given, are a carefully calibrated mirage that doesn't dignify or ennoble but instead sabotages our own sense of ourselves. What's a front and what's real? How might we let a little air in?

EVERYONE'S INVITED

As the essayist Hugh Kenner observes of the forms we honor with the names like art, poetry, gospel or apocalypse, there is always that which "lifts the saying out of the zone of things said."[15] There is always that which puts beauty back in play, making us delight in the possibility of knowing it and calling us back to awareness of ourselves. These are the labors of the ancestors we choose, and they are ours to receive and pass on as the gifts of poetic thinking. This is what the poet Aimé Césaire describes as "that process which through word, image, myth, love, and humor establishes me at the living heart of myself and of the world."[16] We have deep and urgent need of such gifts if we're to be people of the long haul.

"The long haul" is a phrase I associate with Myles Horton of Savannah, Tennessee, teacher and cofounder of the Highlander Folk School. Among the realists of the larger reality I know of, he is one strong link between various figures, artisans of hopefulness in our time, whom we're woefully prone to place in separate eras, concerns and issue-driven camps. The labels, as ever, don't work. They only pervert. Horton studied, learned and strategized, for instance, with Rosa Parks and Dietrich Bonhoeffer, Pete Seeger and Septima Clark, to name a few. In our tendency to elevate individuals as heroes over movements, to the exclusion of the long haul—that slow, communal work of discernment upon which lived righteousness depends—we trade a sense of how we might make ourselves available to history in the here and now for fleeting praise and stunted admiration, words of "due respect" on which we never get around to following through. By only approaching history by way of caricature and "big players," we cut ourselves off from available insight as to how to be available to history now, and the literacy of wonder is lost on us.

Horton, who offered training in nonviolent resistance to Martin Luther King Jr. and John Lewis, believed education is a matter of acquainting people—individuals—with a deeper sense of their own power, their own genius and their revolutionary intuition. He believed we have to credit one another *with* and lift one another *toward* a deeper social acumen and a deeper hungering and thirsting for righteousness than we're accustomed to sensing—than we've been taught to sense—within ourselves:

> I don't think you help people by keeping them enslaved to something that is less than they are capable of doing and believing. I was told one time during an educational conference that I was cruel because I made people who were very happy and contented, unhappy, and that it was wrong to upset people and stretch their imaginations and minds, and to challenge them to the place where they got themselves into trouble, became maladjusted and so on. My position was that I believed in changing society by first changing individuals so that they could then struggle to bring about social changes. There's a lot of pain in it, and a lot of violence, and conflict, and that is just part of the price you pay. I realized that was part of growth—and growth is painful. A plant comes through the hard ground and it breaks the seed apart. And then it dies

to live again. I think that people aren't fully free until they're in a struggle for justice. *And that means for everyone.* It's a struggle of such importance that they are willing, if necessary, to die for it. I think that's what you have to do before you're really free. Then you've got something to live for. You don't want to die, because you've got so much you want to do. The struggle is so important that it gives meaning to life.[17]

So much of what we know and celebrate within the *still-being-realized*, geopolitical revolution referred to as the civil rights movement and that social genius, internationally embodied, that calls itself *beloved community* is evident in this passage. Horton maintained that there is that within every human being which longs for justice and that we aren't quite humanly or humanely literate till that longing becomes embodied in some way, till we enjoin ourselves—our bodies—to the enactment of right order, to the flourishing of others which is ultimately our *own* flourishing. Not a bad vision of the social pipeline. And not a bad way of dwelling most meaningfully within it. Consider the long haul. Everyone's invited.

Everybody I know wants to be true. And despite the fear and the awkwardness, the fronting and the faking, and all the ways we do it badly, I suspect everyone deep down longs to at least pursue the possibility of being genuine. It's so rightly and righteously attractive. Everyone wants to have and dwell within meaning. *Sharing* meaning, though, and *giving* meaning is a slightly different dance from simply expressing your one self. It's funny to put it this way, but you were already doing that. Or as the poet Mary Karr puts it in a little aphorism that sums this book up rather well: "Poetry doesn't need self expression. The self has been expressed. You're standing in it."[18] You're soaking in it. We see and hear you. You can't bring your values—your faith or your supposed non-faith—suddenly into play. That program is already in progress. It was always already there, being voiced. Sometimes louder and sometimes clearer than you intended.

But we can *give* voice anytime at all by listening to someone else, by paying them heed and perhaps trying to do justice to their voice by remembering, rehearsing what we've heard of theirs, with our own. And both paradoxically and maybe a little hilariously, we can't hear our own voice till we've entertained the fact of someone else. Voice doesn't happen in isolation. It can only occur in relationship, the space of the chother, the realm of communion. To be heard at all—to *mean* at all—requires communion.

Perhaps the community you have in view is dysfunctional, broken, embarrassing. Perhaps you have a proposal for it? A word of criticism? Come forth with your critique, but you should know, you can't fix what you won't join. There's no healing a community of which you in no way see yourself a part. Maybe criticism and hospitality can be joined at the hip. Maybe they have to be for a conversation to occur. There are so many ways to weave a common life, to hold together that which is in danger of being *dis*membered. To *re*member, in this sense, is to no longer stand alone and to aid others in no longer doing so. A critique can be a gift, but it need never be confused for a call to abandon the human circle. Are you bewildered? Others have been here before. And at the heart of bewilderment there can be a seed of compassion.

"To what do I appeal when I want to convince myself that I am somebody?" the activist-mystic Howard Thurman once asked his congregation.[19] In what associations do I hope to derive my significance? Both questions speak to the question of communion, those reserves upon which I draw in my attempt to mean well together with others. I have so much, so many ancestors, so many artifacts, to come to my rescue when I sit still long enough to attend to this question.

If I could end—or begin to end—as I began, I'll note again that I'm regularly delivered from certain madness by certain loves. I've shared more than one in the preceding pages. They include very unfamous people, family members, biblical prophets, rebel priests, science-fiction writers, playwrights and all manner of pop-culture artisans. By their lights, I try to love and write the vision, making it as plain as I can, believing that there remains a vision that doesn't lie for any and every time. And with love comes—or can come— what I take to be appropriate anxieties, worries over whether or not I dwell rightly and reverently within a continuum alongside those I love. Would Emily Dickinson find me a little sympathetic and funny? Would James Baldwin think me a tiny bit cool? Would my life make sense to Walt Whitman and the prophet Isaiah? Would Shakespeare spy in me a kindred spirit? This too is a longing for the coherence without which I feel diminished and out of sync. I want to be—to have been—in line with a sacred order. Maybe you do too.

Senses of the sacred differ, but the longing for some form of order is, I think, universal. My favorite thinker in this regard is the poet Gregory Orr, who maintains the following: "Each of us needs to believe that patterns and structures exist and *can be made to exist*. To be human is to have a deep craving for order."[20] We crave— sometimes righteously and sometimes wickedly—order. We expend entire lives in this hope. It's what we do.

I DON'T WANT COMMUNION

As I've mentioned, I've spent thousands of hours of my own life undertaking this ordering attempt in the buildings popularly referred to as churches. For much of my adult life, I've pulled my children along too. As a child, I used to stare at a white wall a few feet away from the preacher and attempt to redeem the time by whiling away the minutes trying to reimagine every last detail of the last movie I'd seen. This, it seemed to me, was an acceptable expenditure of imagination so long as I was there, trying to feel it, trying to be present to the communion that is the trying-to-be-faithful people whose life is *church* and which is from time to time housed in the church *building*. My children pass notes and draw on the bulletins with me, often suddenly require bathroom breaks and roll their eyes at me as I whisper-hiss at them to pay attention. In one such instance, I even placed my fingers on my son Sam's lips to get him to move his mouth to the words of a hymn we were singing. My brother leaned forward from behind us to say, "Tell your dad he needs to behave in church." I considered retorting that I'm never *not* trying to behave in church . . . or *as* church, but I kept it to myself.

Anyway, one recent Sunday, both sons having ducked out to supposedly use the bathroom, Sam appeared with a Dr Pepper he'd procured with change he had, unbeknownst to me, in his jacket pocket. I told him to finish it outside as quickly as he could and to then get his body back in there. The sermon was almost over. After the sermon concluded and Communion was underway, Peter—that bright articulator of the chother principle, whose middle name (wait for it . . .) is Berrigan—made his way down the pew with a plaintive look. "Could I have fifty cents?" he ask-whispered.

"No," I mouthed. He'd seen Sam in the company of a soft drink and thought it only fair that he be accorded one as well. "We'll talk about it later."

"Please," he whispered.

"Save it," I said. "We're about to have Communion."

"I don't want Communion," he decreed in a wide-eyed whisper.

He immediately understood he'd crossed a certain line as sacred to me as any coin flip. No sense in being a silent prophet to my own child. "You and I need to have a conversation." I told him that if he didn't *want* Communion, I'd like for him to wait outside.

Was this me being goofy and mean? Does Peter have a religious nut for a father? Does Communion have to be *wanted* to be rightly entered into or partaken? Am I still the anxious pilgrim in the

Kroger parking lot, wolfing down crackers and grape juice the better to somehow please—and stave off the everlasting wrath of— the Lord? What's the big deal?

It's still a big deal. Peter said he was sorry. I hugged him. And we had a longish conversation about being the people of God and the meaning of Jesus' obedience to God in word and deed, in life and in death, that he likely won't remember. I wanted him to feel zero shame—no interest at all in passing that on—but I desperately hope he'll remain steadfast—and I believe he will—in the way of the gift— the gifts of God for the people of God and the gift *of* God that is the sweet social fact of other people. Estrangement and bewilderment there will doubtless be, but I don't want him to think there's ever any life-giving standing to the side of these gifts. I want him to perceive and receive the gift with all that he is. I want him to know and experience *himself* as gift.

I want my kids to know what they're doing. And if they're destined to live in an often horrifically incurious age, I want them to be part of that peculiarly curious remnant upon whom little or nothing is lost, who love their chother as themselves and who are purposefully lost in admiration for the beauty of the earth that affords them a living. I want them to *know joy*. If all goes as well as I hope it will, I'll learn it from them as much as—probably more than—they'll learn it from me, but my hope is that they'll grow in their love for "the felt fact," Susan Howe's phrase,[21] in all that they're up to and that it will guide their devotion in all the forms it takes.

Our devotion, after all, *takes form*. We're standing in it, walking through it, breathing it, holding it. What shall we do with it? Is it worthy? What form shall my devotion take today? The invitation to the Lord's table (bread or crackers, wine or grape juice) is an invitation to remember well and righteously and specifically, to be among the most specific people the world has ever seen, to imagine ourselves and others poetically and gratefully. And it isn't, in the popular and narrow sense, a *spiritual* vision of the world that's expected to be detached from the actual world. It's a vision that reflects the knowledge of the Lord which, we are told, is to be present to and for the world just as water is present to the sea. It is to be carried over into everything. The Eucharist, we understand, means "thanksgiving." And it seems to me that there is no deep access to life without gratitude. No right perception without the sense of connection and interdependence that necessitates gratitude. The Eucharist is one essential vision of how we might hopefully inhabit the world. I, for one, depend on it.

Love Is Intelligence

To see the world as rigorously liturgical is to see it through the lens of relationship and with an eye on everything that is otherwise trivialized and degraded, to be alive to our own liturgies locally *and* globally. Look around for a screen, a billboard or a conversation overheard, and you may well hear the call to pay no attention to the man behind the curtain, the call to live in denial of relationship to the room, house, neighborhood, city, country or world within which you live and move and have your being. But to live in such denial is to live in diminishment. It is to cut yourself off from your own life.

It's in the hope of resisting this widespread diminishing move that I propose a break with the denial strategy when it comes to religion (religion as thine but never mine), this unfortunate way of distinguishing oneself from others. My assertion that life is too short to pretend we're not religious is largely grounded in the hope that we would come to habitually view relationship—interrelation— as a fact and not an issue. The ancient intelligence available to us in the stories of sacred traditions—we can call them myths so long as doing so doesn't deprive us of our sense of their investigative heft— presumes interrelation at every turn, but one reason we're lately so estranged from this intelligence is our knee-jerk denial of our religiosity, our own fellow humanness. If we think of relation as the starting point of our politics, our policies and the visions for how we mean to organize our lives and our resources, a gust of justice often follows. It is with this insight in mind that the German theologian-activist Dorothee Soelle reminds us that "the relationship between human beings is not to be understood merely as a possibility that is realized now & then."[22] It's rather a fact—the fact—to be lived into at all times. We get to operate out of the blessed realization that "the ego is not the final horizon of the self."[23] It isn't a matter of making such connections; it's the essential task of learning to see, in all things, the fact of connection. The fact, lest we forget, doesn't require our recognition.

Separation, as we've noted, is a sham, but what is more it is an unlovely and unpoetic way of viewing and proceeding with our lives. This brings us back to that place of finding others beautiful and interesting. It often seems to me that such moments don't work *as* work or tasks or anything borne of a sense of obligation. It has to just happen in a gasp of recognition, of empathy, and the difficult joy—it will often have to involve laughter—of realizing how much of what we thought we knew for sure and had squared away was exceedingly wrong. Wrong because we had yet to begin to see with the eyes of love.

The poet Robin Blaser argues that there is no seeing, no understanding without it: "I don't think intelligence exists without love. Love is intelligence. What kind of intelligence would you have without love?"[24] It's love that makes it possible for us to look deep into the eyes of others and see ourselves, our chother, the deep awareness of relationship that puts the mind in full flower and gives rise to the compassion without which there is no hope.

This has been—or I hope it's been—the start of a whisper campaign. We get to unlearn—it seems to me we *have to* unlearn—the habitual defensiveness that only ascribes religiousness to others. And along this trajectory, I call myself religious in an effort to be more exactingly honest with myself concerning what I'm up to. I'm never not worshiping. I'm never not confessing my faith in one way or another. And, if I may be permitted a return to the plural, understanding ourselves to be just as religious as any and everyone else might afford us time, space and vision with which to see ourselves more clearly and honestly, the better to grasp or begin to grasp—it's a life's work after all—the deepest implications of what we're doing to ourselves and others.

This kind of self-understanding can clear a path toward the joys of conversion. Not once-for-all, as if that would be interesting at all, but rather in finding ourselves born again and again toward that literacy of wonder we lose when we're primarily guided by fear and defensiveness and the lazy drive to disassociation—a literacy we begin to achieve anew when affinity, affection and a sense of mutuality guide us in our regard for other people. The joy of a changed mind, that new birth many of us are secretly hoping for most of the time, is often extremely nearby. It might be one conversation, one human face, away. It's never too late to act on the hope you have.

Acknowledgments

WRITE WHAT WILL STOP YOUR BREATH if you don't write," Grace Paley once advised. And I've found it takes a fellowship of curious people (at least one or two) to become and stay motivated in the direction of really doing it. So many sweet people have been consistently kind and inquisitive in helping me to lift up, articulate and generally stick with what's often felt like nothing more than an odd little quibble over an unfashionable and off-putting word. To family and friends and faculty colleagues polite enough to sit still and listen as I tried to explain what I'm on about, I thank you. To students at the Tennessee Prison for Women, Riverbend Maximum Security Institution, Charles B. Bass Correctional Complex, Belmont, Tennessee State, Lipscomb and Vanderbilt University, I thank you for letting me know when I wasn't making any helpful sense and inviting me to try again and again. And for very specific help with the manuscript, I thank Carlene Bauer (whose exceedingly helpful questions gave me a title), J. T. Daly, David Zimmerman, Amy Caldwell and my friends in the Virginia Seminar in Lived Theology: Valerie Cooper, Shannon Gayk, Amy Laura Hall, Susan Holman, Russell Jeung, John Kiess, Jenny McBride, Charles Marsh, Vanessa Ochs, Peter Slade and Shea Tuttle. I also want to communicate my gratitude to Greg Daniel, my agent, and Helen Lee, my editor, for encouraging me to make the time to write my mind the way I want it to read.

Notes

INTRODUCTION: RELIGION HAPPENS

[1] David Byrne, *Bicycle Diaries* (New York: Viking Penguin, 2009), 2.

[2] Elaine Scarry, *On Beauty and Being Just* (Princeton, NJ: Princeton University Press, 1999), 7.

[3] Iris Murdoch, "The Sublime and the Good," in Peter Conradi, ed., *Existentialists and Mystics: Writings on Philosophy and Literature* (New York: Penguin, 1997), 215. With thanks to Sallie McFague for the tip.

CHAPTER 1: CRACKERS AND GRAPE JUICE

[1] Neil Gaiman, *American Gods* (New York: HarperCollins, 2011), 450.

[2] Teresa K. Weaver, "Maya Angelou's final chapter," Palm Beach Post-Cox News Service, May 5, 2002, www.racematters.org/mayaangeloufinal chapter.htm.

CHAPTER 2: ATTENTION COLLECTION

[1] Albert Camus, *The Fall*, trans. Justin O'Brien (New York: Vintage, 1991), 111.

CHAPTER 3: CHOOSE YOUR ANCESTORS CAREFULLY

[1] The skit was written by Adam McKay, who would go on to direct Ferrell in *Anchorman*.

[2] Ralph Ellison, *Shadow and Act* (New York: Random House, 1964), 145. This insight was conveyed to me with enlivening clarity by my mentor Hortense Spillers.

[3] Ibid., 31.

[4] Kurt Vonnegut, introduction to *Mother Night* (New York: Random House, 1966).

[5] I borrow this way of putting it from Sam Dark's elaboration on Shakespeare's counsel from Sonnet 35.

[6] David Gates, "Dylan Revisited," *Newsweek*, October 5, 1997, www .newsweek.com/dylan-revisited-174056.

[7]Mary Rose O'Reilly, *The Barn at the End of the World* (Minneapolis: Milkweed Editions, 2000), 151.

[8]Marilynne Robinson, *Gilead* (New York: Picador, 2004), 114.

[9]John Darnielle, *Wolf in White Van* (New York: Farrar, Straus and Giroux, 2014), 99.

[10]Ibid., 200.

[11]Ibid., 132.

[12]Ibid., 36.

[13]Ibid., 22-23.

[14]Ibid., 195-97.

CHAPTER 4: I LEARNED IT BY WATCHING YOU

[1]William Pietz, "Problem of the Fetish, IIIa," *Res* 16 (Autumn 1988): 112.

[2]"Rod Serling," *American Masters,* December 29, 2003, www.pbs.org /wnet/americanmasters/episodes/rod-serling/about-rod-serling/702/.

[3]Theodore Sturgeon, *More Than Human* (New York: Farrar, Straus and Giroux, 1953), 129.

[4]Ibid., 181.

[5]Ibid., 183.

[6]Ursula K. Le Guin, *The Wind's Twelve Quarters: Short Stories* (New York: Harper and Row, 1975), 285.

[7]Ursula K. Le Guin, *Dispossessed* (New York: Avon, 1974), 84.

[8]Ibid., 247.

[9]Ibid., 47.

[10]Philip K. Dick, *The Shifting Realities of Philip K. Dick: Selected Literary and Philosophical Writings,* ed. Lawrence Sutin (New York: Vintage, 1996), 261.

[11]Philip K. Dick, *The Transmigration of Timothy Archer* (New York: Simon & Schuster, 1982), 55.

[12]Philip K. Dick, *The Three Stigmata of Palmer Eldritch* (New York: Doubleday, 1965), 36-37.

[13]Octavia E. Butler, *Kindred* (Boston: Beacon, 1979), 17.

[14]Ibid., 18.

[15]Ibid., 134.

CHAPTER 5: HURRY UP AND MATTER!

[1]William Wordsworth, *Preface to "Lyrical Ballads,"* www.bartleby .com/39/36.html. I owe my alertness to this application of this passage to

Denis Donoghue, *On Eloquence* (New Haven, CT: Yale University Press, 2008), 11-12.

[2]Jacques Ellul, *The Technological Bluff*, trans. Geoffrey W. Bromiley (Grand Rapids: Eerdmans, 1990), 364.

[3]Larry Rosen, "Multitasking Madness," *Psychology Today*, February 7, 2011, www.psychologytoday.com/blog/rewired-the-psychology -technology/201102/multitasking-madness.

[4]Stephen King, *Cell* (New York: Simon & Schuster, 2006), 329.

[5]James Gibbons, "Beyond Recognition," *Bookforum*, Sept/Oct/Nov 2006, www.bookforum.com/inprint/013_03/555.

[6]Quoted in John Madera, "O For a Muse of Fire . . . An Interview with Lance Olsen," *Rain Taxi*, Online Edition: Summer 2010, www.raintaxi .com/o-for-a-muse-of-fire-an-interview-with-lance-olsen/.

[7]William Stafford, interview by Jeff Gundy, *Artful Dodge*, College of Wooster, OH, http://artfuldodge.sites.wooster.edu/content/conversation -william-stafford.

[8]William Gibson, *Distrust That Particular Flavor* (New York: Penguin, 2012), 44.

[9]Patton Oswalt, "Wake Up, Geek Culture. Time to Die," *Wired*, December 27, 2010, www.wired.com/2010/12/ff_angrynerd_geekculture/all/.

[10]I owe this articulation to Rob and Kirstin Vander Giessen-Reitsma, the founders of *culture is not optional. The community they cultivate and sustain by way of the Huss Project in Three Rivers, Michigan, is, to my mind, an exemplary instance of God's good work.

CHAPTER 6: THE WEB, THE NET AND THE VERSE

[1]"'Nones' on the Rise," Pew Research Center, October 9, 2012, www .pewforum.org/2012/10/09/nones-on-the-rise/.

[2]"Geoffrey Hill, The Art of Poetry No. 80," by Carl Phillips, *The Paris Review* (Spring 2000). www.theparisreview.org/interviews/730/the-art -of-poetry-no-80-geoffrey-hill.

[3]Stan Lee and Steve Ditko, "The Possessed!," *Strange Tales* 118 (March 1964), collected in *Marvel Masterworks* (volume 1), http://marvel.wikia .com/wiki/Strange_Tales_Vol_1_118.

[4]Flannery O'Connor, *Mystery and Manners: Occasional Prose* (New York: Farrar, Straus and Giroux, 2000), 200.

[5]Martin Luther King Jr., "Letter from a Birmingham Jail," April 16, 1963,

audio letter, Stanford University, https://kinginstitute.stanford.edu /king-papers/documents/letter-birmingham-jail.

[6]Marilynne Robinson, *Gilead* (New York: Picador, 2004), 66.

[7]Wendell E. Berry, "It All Turns on Affection," (National Endowment for the Humanities 2012 Jefferson Lecture), www.neh.gov/about/awards /jefferson-lecture/wendell-e-berry-lecture.

[8]Wendell Berry, "Two Economies," World Wisdom Online Library, www .worldwisdom.com/public/viewpdf/default.aspx?article-title=Two _Economies_by_Wendell_Berry.pdf.

[9]Henry David Thoreau, *Walking*, Thoreau Reader, part 1, http://thoreau .eserver.org/walking1.html.

[10]James 1:27.

[11]"Vincent Harding—Civility, History, and Hope," *On Being with Krista Tippett*, May 22, 2014, www.onbeing.org/program/civility-history-and -hope/79.

[12]Desmond Tutu, *No Future Without Forgiveness* (New York: Doubleday, 1999), 31. The germ of this chapter, a welcome intersection of the insights of Wendell Berry and Desmond Tutu, came to me through an unpublished essay by Jacob Harris, an incarcerated philosopher and activist who resides in the Turney Center Industrial Complex.

[13]Søren Kierkegaard, *Fear and Trembling*, trans. Walter Lowrie (Princeton, NJ: Princeton University Press, 1968), 21.

CHAPTER 7: THE CHOTHER

[1]George Monbiot, "The Self-Attribution Fallacy," *The Guardian*, November 7, 2011, www.monbiot.com/2011/11/07/the-self-attribution-fallacy/.

[2]Thomas Merton, *Conjectures of a Guilty Bystander* (New York: Doubleday, 2009), 156.

[3]Wendell Berry, "The Responsibility of the Poet," in *What Are People For?* (New York: North Point Press), 90.

[4]Ibid.

[5]*Mishna Avot* 1:14.

[6]This question arose in my failure to adequately paraphrase an insight articulated by Jaron Lanier in *Who Owns the Future?* (New York: Simon & Schuster, 2013), 31.

[7]Daniel Berrigan, *Jeremiah: The World, the Wound of God* (Minneapolis: Fortress, 1999), 23.

[8]Ralph Ellison, *Invisible Man* (New York: Vintage International, 1995), 581.

CHAPTER 8: POLICY IS LITURGY WRIT LARGE

[1]Rebecca Solnit, "Call climate change what it is: violence," *The Guardian*, April 7, 2014, www.theguardian.com/commentisfree/2014/apr/07 /climate-change-violence-occupy-earth.

[2]Sarah Kendzior, "The telegenically dead: Why Israel and its supporters fear Gaza's dead," Aljazeera, August 14, 2014, www.aljazeera.com /indepth/opinion/2014/08/telegenically-dead-20148118231287o982.html.

[3]Teju Cole, Twitter post, twitter.com/tejucole, April 30, 2014, 7:18 a.m.

[4]Daniel Barrigan, quoted in Walter B. Kalaidjian, *Languages of Liberation: The Social Text in Contemporary American Poetry* (New York: Columbia University Press, 1989), 164.

[5]Daniel Berrigan, *Wisdom: The Feminine Face of God* (London: Sheed & Ward, 2002), 61.

[6]Claudia Luther, "Philip F. Berrigan, 79; Priest and Pacifist Who Helped Inspire Vietnam War Protests," *Los Angeles Times*, December 8, 2002, http://articles.latimes.com/2002/dec/08/local/me-berrigan8.

[7]Daniel Berrigan, *To Dwell in Peace: An Autobiography* (San Francisco: Harper & Row, 1987), 201-2.

[8]Ibid.

[9]Ibid., 219-20.

[10]Ibid., 221.

[11]Daniel Berrigan, *Consequences: Truth and . . .* (New York: Macmillan, 1967), 78.

[12]Daniel Berrigan, introduction to *The Time's Discipline: The Beatitudes and Nuclear Resistance*, by Philip Berrigan and Elizabeth McAlister, (Baltimore: Fortkamp, 1989), xx.

[13]Daniel Kreps, "David Byrne Can't Vote But Hopes You Will," *Rolling Stone*, November 4, 2008, www.rollingstone.com/music/news /david-byrne-cant-vote-but-hopes-you-will-20081104.

CHAPTER 9: STRANGE NEGOTIATIONS

[1]Kim Jensen, "Fanny Howe," *BOMB*, Winter 2013, http://bombmagazine .org/article/6925/fanny-howe.

[2]Nathan Schneider, *Thank You, Anarchy: Notes from the Occupy Apocalypse* (Berkeley: University of California Press, 2013), 74.

[3]Ursula Le Guin, "Speech in Acceptance of the National Book Foundation Medal," November 19, 2014, www.ursulakleguin.com/NationalBook FoundationAward-Speech.html. Copyright © 2014 Ursula K. Le Guin.

[4]Daniel Berrigan, *Absurd Convictions, Modest Hopes: Conversations after Prison with Lee Lockwood* (New York: Random House, 1972), 107.

[5]Jaron Lanier, *Who Owns the Future?* (New York: Simon & Schuster, 2013), 14.

[6]Daniel Berrigan, *No Bars to Manhood* (Garden City, NY: Doubleday, 1970), 55.

[7]Daniel Berrigan and Adrianna Amari, *Prayer for the Morning Headlines: On the Sanctity of Life and Death* (Baltimore: Apprentice House, 2007), cover.

[8]Daniel Berrigan, preface to *Suspect Tenderness*, by William Stringfellow and Anthony Towne (New York: Holt, Rinehart, and Winston, 1971), 7.

[9]Stringfellow and Towne, "On Sheltering Criminal Priests," in *Suspect Tenderness*, 22.

[10]Ibid., 31.

[11]Ibid., 48.

[12]Daniel Berrigan, *And the Risen Bread: Selected Poems*, ed. John Dear (New York: Fordham, 1998), 230.

[13]"We translated our ignorance into their pain. That is the story the Senate report tells." Mark Danner and Hugh Eaken, "The CIA: The Devastating Indictment," MarkDanner.com, February 5, 2015, www.markdanner.com /articles/the-cia-the-devastating-indictment.

[14]Daniel Berrigan, "An Ethic of Resurrection," in *Testimony: The Word Made Flesh* (Maryknoll, NY: Orbis, 2004), 220-221.

[15]Hugh Kenner, *A Homemade World: The American Modernist Writers* (New York: Knopf, 1975), 60.

[16]Aimé Césaire, introduction to *Lyric and Dramatic Poetry, 1946-1982*, trans. Clayton Eshleman and Annette Smith (Charlottesville: University Press of Virginia, 1990), lv.

[17]Myles Horton with Judith Kohl and Herbert Kohl, *The Long Haul: An Autobiography* (New York: Teacher's College Press, 1998), 184. I'd like to thank Michael Gagné, who shared this passage with me. Italics mine.

[18]Mary Karr, Twitter post, https://twitter.com/marykarrlit, November 22, 2013, 8:06 a.m.

[19]Howard Thurman, "Barren or Fruitful?," in *A Strange Freedom: The Best*

of Howard Thurman on Religious Experience and Public Life, ed. Walter Earl Fluker and Catherine Tumbler (Boston: Beacon Press, 1999), 23.

[20]Gregory Orr, *Poetry as Survival* (Athens: University of Georgia Press, 2002), 16. Italics mine.

[21]Susan Howe, *Souls of the Labadie Tract* (New York: New Directions, 2007), 9.

[22]Dorothee Soelle, *Mystery of Death,* trans. Nancy and Martin Lukens-Rumscheidt (Minneapolis: Fortress, 2007), 79.

[23]Ibid., 111.

[24]Douglas Todd, "Hippest Man on Earth," *Vancouver Sun,* September 6, 2008, www2.canada.com/vancouversun/news/westcoastnews/story .html?id=7936ead0-aa9e-4c87-a3e0-4c2333e1c564&p=4 Robin Blaser.